Write About Poetry

How do we read poetry, compare poems, or generate observations into a thoughtful response? *Write About Poetry* is an invaluable reference book and skills guide for students of poetry. Featuring model essays, a glossary of technical terms, and additional practice for student engagement, this volume provides students with a clear and concise guide to:

- reading unseen poems with confidence
- developing general observations into formal, structured written responses
- fostering familiarity with some of the great poets and poems in literary history

Drawing on years of teaching experience, Steven Jackson delivers the background, progressive methodology, and practical essay writing techniques essential for understanding the fundamental steps of poetry analysis.

Steven Jackson is an English teacher at Queen Anne's School, Caversham, and is currently Head of Key Stage Three for English. He has also organised several English A-level enrichment programmes, including teaching 'The Forms of Poetry' and 'Scenes from Shakespeare' for English Oxbridge preparation. He has been published in *The English Review*, and as a poet and prize winner at the Brian Dempsey Memorial Competition, the Ver Prize, and Marsden the Poetry Village Competition.

Write About Poetry
Getting to the Heart of a Poem

Steven Jackson

NEW YORK AND LONDON

Cover image: © Getty Images

First published 2022
by Routledge
605 Third Avenue, New York, NY 10158

and by Routledge
2 Park Square, Milton Park, Abingdon, Oxon, OX14 4RN

Routledge is an imprint of the Taylor & Francis Group, an informa business

© 2022 Steven Jackson

The right of Steven Jackson to be identified as author of this work has been asserted in accordance with sections 77 and 78 of the Copyright, Designs and Patents Act 1988.

All rights reserved. No part of this book may be reprinted or reproduced or utilised in any form or by any electronic, mechanical, or other means, now known or hereafter invented, including photocopying and recording, or in any information storage or retrieval system, without permission in writing from the publishers.

Trademark notice: Product or corporate names may be trademarks or registered trademarks, and are used only for identification and explanation without intent to infringe.

Library of Congress Cataloging-in-Publication Data
A catalog record for this title has been requested

ISBN: 978-1-032-07528-0 (hbk)
ISBN: 978-1-032-07527-3 (pbk)
ISBN: 978-1-003-20751-1 (ebk)

DOI: 10.4324/9781003207511

Typeset in Bembo
by Deanta Global Publishing Services, Chennai, India

for Ami and Spencer

Contents

Acknowledgements   viii

Introduction   1

1 Who Is Involved?   4

2 What Is the Situation?   26

3 What Is the Central Theme?   43

4 Practical Criticism and the 5-Part Essay   64

5 Three Essays   75

6 Answering an Essay Question   88

7 Comparing Poems   101

8 Exploring a Group of Poems   126

Afterword   153
Biographies of the Featured Poets   154
Glossary of Key Terms   159
Index   163

Acknowledgements

Poem 'An Unknown Girl' by Moniza Alvi published in *Spilt World: Poems 1990–2005*, Bloodaxe Books, 2007. Reproduced by permission of Bloodaxe Books on behalf of the author, www.bloodaxebooks.com.

Poem 'Zoom!' by Simon Armitage, published in *Zoom!*, Bloodaxe Books, 1989. Reproduced by permission of Bloodaxe Books on behalf of the author, www.bloodaxebooks.com.

Poems 'After great pain, a formal feeling comes', 'I Felt a Funeral, in my Brain', 'It was not for Death for I stood up' and 'There's a certain Slant of Light' by Emily Dickinson, The Poems of Emily Dickinson: Reading Edition, edited by Ralph W. Franklin, Cambridge, Mass.: The Belknap Press of Harvard University Press, Copyright © 1998, 1999 by the President and Fellows of Harvard College. Copyright © 1951, 1955 by the President and Fellows of Harvard College. Copyright © renewed 1979, 1983 by the President and Fellows of Harvard College. Copyright © 1914, 1918, 1919, 1924, 1929, 1930, 1932, 1935, 1937, 1942 by Martha Dickinson Bianchi. Copyright © 1952, 1957, 1958, 1963, 1965 by Mary L. Hampson.

Poem 'Blessing' by Imtiaz Dharker, published in *Postcards from God*, Bloodaxe Books, 1997. Reproduced by permission of Bloodaxe Books on behalf of the author, www.bloodaxebooks.com.

Poem 'Hawk Roosting' by Ted Hughes, from *Lupercal*. Reprinted by permission of Faber & Faber.

Poem 'For a Child Born Dead' by Elizabeth Jennings, from *The Collected Poems by Elizabeth Jennings*, published by Carcanet Press; reproduced by kind permission by David Higham Associates.

Poem 'Wedding' by Alice Oswald, from *The Thing in the Gap Stone Stile*. Reprinted by permission of Faber & Faber.

Poem 'Beehive' by Jean Toomer, 'Jean Toomer Papers, James Weldon Johnson Memorial Collection in the Yale Collection of American Literature, Beinecke Rare Book and Manuscript Library'. Credit line: '(c) Yale University. All rights reserved.

Poems 'The Desolate Field', 'January', 'Complaint', and 'Thursday' by William Carlos Williams, from *The Collected Poems: Volume I, 1909–1939*, copyright ©1938 by New Directions Publishing Corp. Reprinted by permission of New Directions Publishing Corp.

Every effort has been made to trace and contact all copyright holders before publication. If notified we will be pleased to rectify any errors or omissions at the earliest opportunity.

Introduction

Studying poetry can be really challenging.

At some stage throughout our early school years it is inevitable that we will be asked by our English teachers in the classroom to engage with the poems of a famous poet or two, and by the time we reach our GCSE and A-level studies we will probably find that we have already encountered a great range of poems and poets and that we have even begun to write down our responses in the form of essays.

Regardless of a student's interest or disinterest in poetry, its ever-presence in our lives is a fact of our education, from infants learning first nursery rhymes to teenagers on the cusp of choosing A-levels, starting university, or leaving school to enter the world of work.

It's also clear that because the study of poetry has long been an educational requirement in these demanding examination years, for the general student of English the potential for a slightly negative attitude towards the subject can emerge. Often a classroom's universal response to the English teacher's spritely introduction: 'This term, students, we will be studying poetry!' is one of a collective groan. 'Oh no, not POETRY!'

This is a great shame. There can be a lot of pleasure found when reading or studying a new poem if the act of reading or studying a new poem does not feel like a requirement or demand. When reading poetry becomes an end in itself – an action that feels quite natural or instinctive, rather than forced – the subject can be inspiring, motivating, and immediately rewarding. The reading of a single poem could even be life-changing.

This is the attitude that I hope this book will foster in students who are intrigued by poetry, yet who might be wary of and even confused by it at times. I hope that this book will act as a guide in how to read and understand poems with more confidence, and how to put this understanding into words on the written page.

I hope this book will help the general student of poetry to write about poems with growing skill and flair.

DOI: 10.4324/9781003207511-1

Unseen

In the classroom we often use the term 'unseen' for poems which students might never have encountered before, or for poems which are being seen and studied for the first time.

For any student meeting a new poem in this way, it can be a very daunting prospect. There are so many things to consider with a poem, after all: the form, the structure, the stanza patterns, the rhyme scheme, the line lengths, the metaphors (if there are any), the sound effects – the very words themselves!

As a result, it often occurs in the classroom that students are given a whole host of strange and obscure poetic terms to learn, which might mean very little to them in all honesty. And there is a great danger in approaching poems in this way, or in thinking that this is all that matters in the experience of studying poetry.

On first reading a poem, too much focus on these 'poetic techniques' can be a real barrier to understanding and enjoying the poem itself.

When we sit down to read our favourite novels, for example, what do we enjoy most? The general reader might say that it is engaging character descriptions, interesting plot, and memorable moments of action. We don't necessarily fixate on the technicalities of narrative perspective, or deeply question why a writer has used a non-linear plot over more linear sequencing of events, for example, when reading at home. We don't focus on these things when reading for pleasure, because, often, these techniques do not take us closer to 'the heart' of the novel.

So, why do we feel a need to do this with poetry?

It seems to come back to the way poetry is taught for examinations, and the standard idea that students have only been truly successful if they can discuss a range of poetic techniques in their written responses. From experience, this approach has not always resulted in very pleasing essay work, or in proud and empowered students who are inspired by the poems that they have read and explored on the written page.

If we change our instinctive response to reading a new poem for the first time, by focusing less on the techniques at first, and more on getting to 'the heart' of the poem, things become much easier and reading poetry will become less intimidating and, I dare say, more of an habitual pleasure!

The Heart of a Poem

But, in order to get to 'the heart' of a poem, there are a few practical steps a student, or any reader for that matter, can take.

Ultimately, what we should aim to achieve on first reading a new poem is a general understanding of what is actually happening in the poem, and to write these observations down in our own words. We have to create the imaginative space of the poem in our minds, and in order to do so we can try to answer these simple questions: 'Who is involved in the poem?' and 'What is the situation of the poem?'.

Because every poem relies on some sort of narrative voice (a figure we call 'the **speaker**'), we can be confident in the knowledge that nearly every poem will involve a certain person or figure at some point. So, one of our first jobs is to work out who or what the speaker of the poem is and if there are any other people, figures, or voices involved. Then, we can consider the situation of the poem. By situation, we might mean setting or location, or possibly the moment, the scene, or the action of the poem.

With this done, any poem, we will find, will soon open up and reveal itself to us.

1 Who Is Involved?

Take for example, the following poem, 'The Voice', by Thomas Hardy (1840–1920), which was written in 1912:

The Voice

by Thomas Hardy

> Woman much missed, how you call to me, call to me,
> Saying that now you are not as you were
> When you had changed from the one who was all to me,
> But as at first, when our day was fair.
>
> 5 Can it be you that I hear? Let me view you, then,
> Standing as when I drew near to the town
> Where you would wait for me: yes, as I knew you then,
> Even to the original air-blue gown!
>
> Or is it only the breeze, in its listlessness
> 10 Travelling across the wet mead to me here,
> You being ever dissolved to wan wistlessness,
> Heard no more again far or near?
>
> Thus I; faltering forward,
> Leaves around me falling,
> 15 Wind oozing thin through the thorn from norward,
> And the woman calling.

After this first reading, we want to try to understand three things better: Who is the speaker? Who else is involved in the poem? What is the situation of the poem?

The first important words to annotate (to highlight and make note of) are pronouns. Personal **pronouns** are words like 'I', 'me', 'you', 'he', 'she', 'it',

DOI: 10.4324/9781003207511-2

'him', 'her', 'we', 'us' 'you' (in the plural sense), 'they', and 'them'. These are a good starting point, but we can also consider other possessive pronouns like 'my', 'your', 'his', 'her', 'its', 'our', 'your' (in the plural sense), and 'their'. There are many other types of pronouns – but the ones listed will form a good starting point.

Our detective work takes place in the early stages of the poem, typically the first verses (more commonly **stanzas**). We should read carefully the opening parts of the poem and try to piece bits of information together. So, let's begin. Where are the first pronouns?

Let's look at the first stanza:

> Woman much missed, how **you** call to **me**, call to **me**,
> Saying that now **you** are not as **you** were
> When **you** had changed from the one who was all to **me**,
> But as at first, when **our** day was fair.

In the opening line of Hardy's poem, the notable pronouns are the personal pronouns 'you' and 'me'. The 'me' pronoun indicates that the poem is written in the **first-person perspective**. When we evaluate the opening stanza in full and consider the other pronouns or figures involved, we see the pronoun 'you' is used again, twice in fact, on line 2. Reading on we find that 'me' is used again on line 3, but more importantly find that the pronoun 'you' is also used once more. With this series of 'me' and 'you' pronoun combinations we get a sense of a **direct address**, or a feeling that the speaker is talking to another person (technically termed 'the **addressee**') specifically.

By making logical connections in the poem we understand that the 'you' pronoun actually refers to one person specifically: the anonymous 'Woman much missed' who is addressed at the very start, in line 1:

Woman much missed, how **you** call to **me**, call to **me**

Therefore, we can imagine the speaker addressing his words to this one woman in, what some might deem, an intimate or private way. The words of the poem, after all, are ones which appear to be shared between the two figures alone. We get a sense of this intimacy if we look at the next notable pronoun in the poem 'our' – a plural possessive pronoun – which suggests that the two figures once shared a time together in their past in the phrase: 'when **our** day was fair' (line 4).

Still focusing on the first stanza of the poem, more important detective work can be done. We could argue that there is another pronoun present here, or a very revealing reference to another figure, at least. For example, on first reading, did you consider 'the one' as a type of pronoun? Well, yes, it is in a way – here it operates as a singular noun in the same way 'he', 'she', 'it' can be used.

6   *Who Is Involved?*

Let's look at line 3 carefully (the line in which 'the one' occurs) for a moment then:

> When you had changed from **the one** who was all to me

Here, the woman much missed (the 'you' of the poem) is also 'the one' – more importantly, she is 'the one' who has 'changed'; 'the one' who 'was all' to the speaker once before.

We might find now that the poem is already becoming more clear and that what we have, ultimately, is a scene between two central figures in the poem: the speaker and the addressee. We can then specify further and make the assertion that the speaker is a man who addresses a woman with whom he once shared a relationship – a woman whom he admits he misses. The speaker might become, then, in our minds, a melancholic or sad figure, while the addressee, in turn, becomes an absent figure in the poem.

If we continue on in this way and begin to highlight the pronouns in the second stanza, they typically arrive as a series of pairs in the fashion of the first stanza:

> 5   Can it be **you** that **I** hear? Let **me** view **you**, then,
> Standing as when **I** drew near to the town
> Where **you** would wait for **me**: yes, as **I** knew **you** then,
> Even to the original air-blue gown!

Here, we find further combinations of 'me' and 'you' (on line 5); 'me' and 'you' (at the beginning of line 7) and 'I' and 'you' (at the end of line 7). It is becoming clear that Hardy is building the poem around the relationship between these two figures.

With this groundwork completed, we can then focus on trying to understand the situation of the poem more precisely. It is clear that two figures are involved in the poem (the speaker and the woman) but now we need to examine this relationship specifically by reviewing the situation of the poem throughout. It is important to note that the situation of a given poem is not always entirely fixed throughout – the scene, the moment, or the action can potentially change at any stage. Therefore, further careful reading is needed.

For example, at the start of Hardy's poem, the speaker states 'Woman much missed, how you call to me, call to me' and so we might imagine her voice calling to him right from the beginning – we do not hear her exact words, but it is implied in the second line that she is communicating to him directly.

We can then start to comment confidently on some quite difficult passages of the poem, and pay particular attention to how the situation of the poem might change. Like, for example, the question which arrives in the opening of stanza 2: 'Can it be you that I hear?' (line 6). This is perhaps the first potentially confusing line of the poem, but, because we have some understanding of the

Who Is Involved? 7

speaker as a man who has experienced a difficult relationship and a lost love, we can start to contemplate now, as readers, why the speaker asks such a thing and we can question whether the speaker has even heard the woman's voice at all – we may even begin to think he is, in fact, imagining it.

The situation of the poem is therefore drastically changing. We are trying to discover now whether the speaker is in the woman's company at the start of the poem, or whether he is, more probably, alone. Let's keep digging to find out.

As we enter the third stanza, it appears that Hardy changes the situation of the poem further to clarify the scene. For the first time, he gives a clearer sense that the sad speaker *is* alone:

> Or is **it** only the breeze, in **its** listlessness
> 10   Travelling across the wet mead to me here,
> **You** being ever dissolved to wan wistlessness,
> Heard no more again far or near?

The voice and presence of the much missed woman is 'dissolved' (line 11) into nothingness and replaced by the sound of the 'breeze' (line 9). The pronouns in this stanza are also straightforward. 'It' on line 9 refers to the sound of the voice, while 'its' on the same line refers to the breeze here. The 'You' pronoun on line 11 remains consistent as referring to the woman (the addressee). Therefore we can be confident when we state that the phrase 'You being ever dissolved' means that the woman much missed has always ('ever') been absent physically from the action of the poem.

To confirm this, it is interesting how the dominant pronouns in the final stanza are singular pronouns ('I' and 'me' on lines 13 and 14) which once more suggest the isolation of the speaker overall:

> Thus **I**; faltering forward,
> Leaves around **me** falling,
> 15   Wind oozing thin through the thorn from norward,
> And the woman calling.

The only company is the wind and 'the woman calling' – a voice we now know is 'only the breeze' – a voice we now know is imagined by the sad speaker and not real.

So, after all of this hard effort and diligent detective work, we are in a good position to attempt a general summary of the poem:

> **Thomas Hardy's poem 'The Voice' describes a sad, isolated speaker, who longs for a lost love – the 'woman much missed' of the opening line. In the desperate action of the poem, the speaker imagines he**

8   *Who Is Involved?*

> **can hear her voice and feel her presence too. Hardy plays with the reader's understanding, blurring the sense of imagination and reality as the speaker is seen to confuse the voice of his lost love with the sounds of the breeze throughout.**

Just think, after only a quick first reading of the poem, would we have been in a confident enough position to make a summary like this? Probably not. The careful reading and rereading all make this possible.

Let's look at another poem now: a poem entitled 'Conscious' by Wilfred Owen (1893–1918), a poet of the First World War. Some might argue that this is a more challenging piece, in terms of trying to understand clearly the speaker and the other voices involved in the action of the poem.

Conscious

by Wilfred Owen

    His fingers wake, and flutter up the bed.
    His eyes come open with a pull of will,
    Helped by the yellow may-flowers by his head.
    The blind-cord drawls across the window-sill…
5   What a smooth floor the ward has! What a rug!
    Who is that talking somewhere out of sight?
    Three flies are creeping round the shiny jug…
    "Nurse! Doctor!"—"Yes, all right, all right."

    But sudden evening muddles all the air—
10 There seems no time to want a drink of water.
    Nurse looks so far away. And here and there
    Music and roses burst through crimson slaughter.
    He can't remember where he saw blue sky.
    More blankets. Cold. He's cold. And yet so hot.
15 And there's no light to see the voices by…
    There is no time to ask—he knows not what.

What a dramatic poem! But let's try to understand it better. Again, we often find that a lot of the detective work takes place in the early phases of a poem, so let us start here. Let's look at the opening stanza and find the first pronouns. Where are they exactly?

    His fingers wake, and flutter up the bed.
    His eyes come open with a pull of will,

Helped by the yellow may-flowers by **his** head.
The blind-cord drawls across the window-sill . . .
5   What a smooth floor the ward has! What a rug!
Who is that talking somewhere out of sight?
Three flies are creeping round the shiny jug...
"Nurse! Doctor!"—"Yes, all right, all right."

Interestingly, the very first word from the opening line of Owen's poem is a pronoun: 'His'. So we know that there is someone (an anonymous man in this case) who is involved in the poem. The same pronoun, 'His', is repeated at the start of the second line, so we have a clear subject focus for the poem: this anonymous male figure. We have another 'his' on line 3 and at this stage we are safe to assume that this is the same man as mentioned before because we have had no indication of anyone else present in the poem yet.

Where, though, is the next important pronoun? Who else is involved?

Well, there is something interesting happening on line 6. We have an indication of another voice: of a hidden person 'talking somewhere out of sight'. So, we now know that the figure in the poem is not alone.

This is revealed further on line 8. This is such an important line because we have two voices in **direct speech** here (note the speech marks) separated by a dash in the middle:

"Nurse! Doctor!"—"Yes, all right, all right."

The first voice (we might assume it is the anonymous man who is the subject of the poem) cries '"Nurse! Doctor!"'. And we hear a voice in response: '"Yes, all right, all right."'

So we have even more people involved in the poem now. But, who is the second voice that speaks the line: '"Yes, all right, all right"'? Is it the Nurse or Doctor? Take a moment and logically decide. The clues (the answers really) are right there in the poem. Consider the reason why it is most logically the Nurse. She is mentioned in the second stanza on line 11: 'Nurse looks so far away'; however, the Doctor is not mentioned again in the poem. Also, the **tone** of her voice is a frustrated, impatient one. The repetition of 'all right, all right' suggests this, and therefore her frustrations match with the distant image of her being 'so far away' and out of reach.

If we finish by highlighting our remaining pronouns, we can see a pattern forming. Owen closes the poem by focusing again on the anonymous man in the final stanza:

But sudden evening muddles all the air—
10   There seems no time to want a drink of water.
Nurse looks so far away. And here and there
Music and roses burst through crimson slaughter.

10   *Who Is Involved?*

>   **He** can't remember where **he** saw blue sky.
>   More blankets. Cold. **He**'s cold. And yet so hot.
> 15 And there's no light to see the voices by…
>   There is no time to ask—**he** knows not what.

'He' is referred to in lines 13, 14, and 16 (the final line of the poem). So, after all of this groundwork and close observation of pronouns we know that the anonymous man is the focus of the piece. After this, we are in a good position to summarise and keep the poem as a whole clearly in mind.

Now, we know that the poem includes description of a number of people: the anonymous man; the voice from the person who is 'somewhere out of sight'; definitely the Nurse; possibly the Doctor. But, we are left to ask – who, therefore, is the speaker? If we compare this poem with the Hardy poem studied before, we will find that the speaker of the poem is far less obvious. In Hardy's poem the speaker was clearly indicated by the first-person pronouns 'I' and 'me'. In Owen's poem here, the first-person pronouns do not exist. This poem is written in the **third-person narrative perspective** because the subject of the poem is written using the third-person personal pronouns: 'He' and 'His'.

However, this does not mean that there is no speaker-figure in the poem. Instead, what we find when poems employ a third-person perspective is that the speaker becomes a sort of commentator figure – a reporter on or overseer of events in the poem. This is a good way of summarising the speaker of this poem. In 'Conscious' the speaker is the commentator of the scene through whose eyes we see the other figures and the situation of the poem. Sometimes the speaker of a poem written in the third person will be objective and emotionally detached; however, in other poems, the speaker is a character themselves and their distinctive voice or subjective opinion can be heard.

What might we say about the speaker in Owen's poem then? Let's quickly consider the situation of the poem and then we can make a clear summary.

If we read carefully, we have obvious clues also about the situation of the poem. Revealing words like 'bed', 'may-flowers', 'blind-cord', 'window-sill', 'ward', 'Nurse', 'Doctor', and 'blankets' should be highlighted and their associated sense should help us imagine clearly a hospital setting. When we reread the opening stanza and make further connections, we can confidently assume that the subject of the poem (the anonymous man) is a sick patient, waking up in his hospital bed at the start.

We can then return to the speaker of the poem and speculate on his role or position in the poem – given the hospital setting, and the fact that the speaker is in the scene making observations about the sick patient, we might imagine that the speaker is a fellow patient, or a helper on the ward, a doctor or even another nurse. Some might argue that, because we get the sense of the inner workings of the patient's mind, the speaker *is* the patient himself and the poem is written from some detached, strange, outer-body perspective. Who knows? With the third-person perspective, there is even the sense that we, the reader, are present in the scene, making these observations ourselves through the lens of Owen's speaker.

We will never know for certain, but this is the brilliance of Owen's poem – we are left to imagine and complete our own picture of the scene.

So, perhaps we have done enough detective work. Now let's ask ourselves – are we in a position to summarise the poem? Who is the speaker? Who is involved? What is the situation of the poem?

> **In 'Conscious' by Wilfred Owen we see, through the commentary of his third-person speaker, a description of a bleak hospital setting and the suffering and confused state of one particular sick and desperate patient throughout. We get a sense of this patient's isolation on the ward, and his possible neglect at the hands of the impatient, unfeeling Nurse, which forms the unsettling mood of the poem overall.**

Think again – after only one, quick reading of the poem, would we have been in a position to make a summary of this kind? Remember, by carefully rereading the poem again and again with a focus on pronouns, the speaker, the people involved, the situation and the setting, you will get closer to 'the heart' of the poem every time.

We are now ready to consider another Thomas Hardy poem – one which has a very clear and obvious speaker, but ambiguous and potentially confusing pronouns. This is a good poem to use as a study or exercise in this case. The poem is called 'The Darkling Thrush' and was written in 1900:

The Darkling Thrush

by Thomas Hardy

    I leant upon a coppice gate
        When Frost was spectre-grey,
    And Winter's dregs made desolate
        The weakening eye of day.
5   The tangled bine-stems scored the sky
        Like strings of broken lyres,
    And all mankind that haunted nigh
        Had sought their household fires.

    The land's sharp features seemed to be
10 The Century's corpse outleant,
    His crypt the cloudy canopy,
        The wind his death-lament.

12   *Who Is Involved?*

> The ancient pulse of germ and birth
>   Was shrunken hard and dry,
> 15 And every spirit upon earth
>   Seemed fervourless as I.
>
> At once a voice arose among
>   The bleak twigs overhead
> In a full-hearted evensong
> 20   Of joy illimited;
> An aged thrush, frail, gaunt, and small,
>   In blast-beruffled plume,
> Had chosen thus to fling his soul
>   Upon the growing gloom.
>
> 25 So little cause for carolings
>   Of such ecstatic sound
> Was written on terrestrial things
>   Afar or nigh around,
> That I could think there trembled through
> 30   His happy good-night air
> Some blessed Hope, whereof he knew
>   And I was unaware.

In our usual style, after the initial reading, let's re-examine the first stanza and try to get a picture of what is happening.

If we search through the early parts of 'The Darkling Thrush', we find that the speaker and situation of the poem are clearly revealed. We should also probably note that the first four lines essentially establish the scene of the poem. This is interesting because it is at the end of the first four lines where we find the first full stop in the poem:

> I leant upon a coppice gate
>   When Frost was spectre-grey,
> And Winter's dregs made desolate
>   The weakening eye of day.

And this brings us on to another important step that we should consider when trying to understand a poem better for the first time: always look for the full stops and always read 'to' the punctuation throughout. This prevents us from unnaturally stopping at the end of each line as if the sentence ends there. As a rule, we find that we can achieve much better sense of the lines and what is going on if we treat them as **verse paragraphs** or in their '**sentence sense**' rather than as individual lines. Experienced readers of poetry always read through the lines to the full stops because, rarely, we find, does a line make sense on its own.

As mentioned then, if we look at Hardy's poem, the first full stop is used at the end of line 4, and essentially, we can write out these lines to make one sentence with a complete sense:

> **I leant upon the coppice-gate when frost was spectre-grey and winter's dregs made desolate the weakening eye of day.**

Bar the inverted **syntax** of 'winter's dregs made desolate the weakening eye of day' (which for greater clarity can be reordered and understood as: 'winter's dregs made the weakening eye of day desolate'), the sentence is straightforward and clear.

The first pronoun in the poem is actually the first word: 'I', so immediately we know we have a first-person speaker who becomes the voice of the poem, and as we finish reading the simple sentence we know the location and action of the speaker and the season too – he is leaning on the gate of a coppice (an area of woodland) in winter.

No alarms and no surprises here.

As we continue to search for the pronouns in the opening stanza, we find the next one is straightforward too:

5   The tangled bine-stems scored the sky
      Like strings of broken lyres,
    And all **mankind** that haunted nigh
      Had sought **their** household fires

In the final two lines of the stanza: 'And all mankind that haunted nigh / Had sought their household fires' (lines 7 and 8), we see the plural pronoun 'their' logically refers to 'mankind' – or in other words the people who have decided to stay in their homes by their fires on this grey, winter's evening.

Therefore we can summarise the opening stanza:

> **In Hardy's 'The Darkling Thrush' the speaker is leaning on a gate by a wood in a grey, winter setting. It is a bleak, rural scene, and Hardy implies that the solitary speaker is the only person out and about as the night draws in.**

However, it is the moment when we turn to the second stanza, that unclear and ambiguous pronouns create a bit of confusion. It is here where things can

14 *Who Is Involved?*

become slightly tricky, but let's slow down and try to read as carefully as possible. Let's look at the second stanza in isolation:

> The land's sharp features seemed to be
> 10   The Century's corpse outleant,
>   **His** crypt the cloudy canopy,
>   The wind **his** death-lament.
>   The ancient pulse of germ and birth
>   Was shrunken hard and dry,
> 15 And every spirit upon earth
>   Seemed fervourless as **I**.

Now, let's find the pronouns in this stanza and discuss. The next one is a possessive pronoun 'His' and appears in the noun phrase: 'His crypt' (line 11). So, we are probably left thinking, whose crypt is this? We see another possessive pronoun on the following line in the phrase: 'his death-lament' (line 12). We have to read very carefully to work out the 'sentence sense' of this part of the poem and then we can examine who (or what) the 'his' pronoun refers to.

Essentially, we are trying to find the subject of this sentence – the subject of these lines in the poem. Also, if we look out for the full stop, we find that line 9 to line 12 forms the next full sentence. So, let's rewrite it (for our own sake) to make it clearer on the page. It becomes:

> **The land's sharp features seemed to be the Century's corpse outleant – his crypt [was] the cloudy canopy; the wind [was] his death-lament.**

As you might see, I have changed the punctuation of the poem (using a dash and semi-colon in place of commas) so that the sentence makes more sense grammatically. Also, for clarity, I have imagined the missing verb ('was') to be in place. This helps further with understanding the grammar of the sentence.

Now, when we evaluate this as a clear sentence, it seems the pronoun 'his' can refer to either 'the land's sharp features' or to 'the Century's corpse'. We should ask ourselves which is the more logical subject for the pronoun of these two, and there are some clues which will help us find the answer.

First, we must consider that the pronoun 'his' suggests possession by a male figure. Remember, our phrase is 'his crypt' and, therefore, the possession in question here is a 'crypt' or tomb – a place in which to rest a dead body. And so, if we look at the two possible subjects in this sentence, the crypt is most logically going to belong to a corpse: here then, we must consider 'the Century's corpse' as the entity which owns or possesses the crypt in question.

To confirm this, we can also safely assume in this instance that it is 'the Century's corpse' that is referred to by the pronoun 'his' because of Hardy's use of a capital letter for 'Century'. A tradition in poetry was to **personify** (give human characteristics to) abstract notions like Love, Time, and Death in this way. (A good poem to consider is Shakespeare's 'Sonnet 116' which personifies both Love and Time, making them seemingly 'human' figures in his poem). A capital letter for such terms suggests that they are living, breathing, thinking entities, and Hardy does this here with the passing century. For Hardy, 'The Century' becomes human metaphorically. More specifically, it becomes a 'corpse' of a human – a life that has passed away.

We are in a position to summarise therefore and say that Hardy's **metaphors** for death show how the century's dead body is evident in 'the land's sharp features'; its tomb is seen in the dark skies ('the cloudy canopy') overhead, and the mournful song ('the death-lament') of the wind acts as its funeral song. The signs of death and grief for the lost century are, therefore, present in the landscape of the natural world. We can understand why Hardy might do this in order to bring a mournful tone into the poem – the dawn of a new century is a significant sign of getting older and a stark reminder of a life and time that has passed away and gone for good, after all.

Now, we might think that this was a lot of work, just to discover that no new human figure or person has really been introduced into the action of the poem. However, it is so important that we do this in-depth study of difficult pronouns to understand some of the real complexities of the poem. Perhaps, through this investigation, we have got to 'the heart' of this poem, because we have potentially unearthed a central theme or idea: that of the poet's reaction to passing time, old and new centuries, and a contemplation of the natural world.

No effort or time spent discussing the minute details of a poem is wasted, therefore!

And, if we turn back to our examination of the pronouns in this stanza, we find, on line 16, we have the next pronoun 'I'. In this passage of the poem the speaker confesses to being 'fervourless' (line 16), and here we have a revelation of the speaker's weariness and lifelessness. The bleak mood of Hardy's poem is channelled through the fatigue and woe of the speaker in this case and matches fittingly with the death of the last Century. All is melancholic and sombre at this stage.

Now, however, let's clarify the rest of the poem, and build a fuller summary.

Let's explore the remaining pronouns and examine whether the situation of the poem changes as we read on.

> At once a voice arose among
>   The bleak twigs overhead
> In a full-hearted evensong
> 20   Of joy illimited;
> An aged thrush, frail, gaunt, and small,
>   In blast-beruffled plume,

16 *Who Is Involved?*

>Had chosen thus to fling **his** soul
>   Upon the growing gloom.

It is clear now that the situation of the poem changes dramatically in stanza 3 as Hardy does in fact introduce a new figure into the action. We hear 'a voice' (line 17) and read on to find that it belongs to 'an aged thrush' (line 21). So, at this stage in our reading, we should have a picture of the scene in mind – of Hardy's weary speaker who is alone out in the winter countryside, feeling sorrowful about the passing century and who is suddenly accompanied by the song of a bird. The speaker and the thrush, therefore, are the two central figures in this poem.

In this stanza, the thrush really becomes the focus for the poem and the next pronoun is the word 'his' on line 23 in the phrase: 'his soul'. And, if we read back through the lines carefully, paying attention to the punctuation and the 'sentence sense' of the lines, we find that 'his' clearly refers to the 'soul' (or the spirit) of the old thrush.

We can then evaluate the last stanza and note the pronouns further:

>25 So little cause for carolings
>   Of such ecstatic sound
>   Was written on terrestrial things
>   Afar or nigh around,
>   That **I** could think there trembled through
>30   **His** happy good-night air
>   Some blessed Hope, whereof **he** knew
>   And **I** was unaware.

Hardy brings the poem to a conclusion by creating a contrast between the man and the bird. We find that 'I' and 'his' pronouns are used on lines 29 to 30 respectively, and 'he' and 'I' pronouns are used on lines 31 and 32 to show the relationship between the two figures. Hardy's last lines indicate the difference between them, and if we look to create a 'sentence sense' out of the last four lines we can rewrite the poem in this way:

> **I could think there trembled through his [the old thrush's] happy good-night air [song] some blessed hope, whereof he knew and I was unaware.**

The speaker admits that he cannot sense the hope for the future that the old thrush obviously can. The beauty of the bird's song is alive and full of joy, after all, as seen in the description: 'his happy, good-night air'.

So, we have found after all of this, that the situation of the poem changes significantly throughout. We are introduced to a new figure halfway through the poem and find that both the tone and message of the poem change in the second half of the poem too. With these changes in mind, we can now develop our early summary of the poem. We can refine it much more to factor in the entire poem:

> **In Hardy's 'The Darkling Thrush' the speaker is leaning on a gate by a wood in a grey, winter setting. It is a bleak, rural scene, and Hardy implies that the solitary speaker is the only person out and about as the night draws in. The poem seems to contemplate ideas of how time passes swiftly and how one century turns quickly into another. However, Hardy, by introducing the bright, spirited symbol of the darkling thrush into the poem, shows how there is still hope for the future to come.**

This is a succinct, yet full summary of the poem. Here, we have moved beyond just information about the figures involved and the situation or action of the poem – we have started also to consider central themes and big ideas too!

But, perhaps an even more challenging piece is another of Wilfred Owen's poems, entitled 'Inspection.' This one has a number of voices and figures involved:

Inspection

by Wilfred Owen

"You! What d'you mean by this?" I rapped.
"You dare come on parade like this?"
"Please, sir, it's –" "Old yer mouth," the sergeant snapped.
"I takes 'is name, sir?" – 'Please, and then dismiss.'

5 Some days 'confined to camp' he got,
For being 'dirty on parade'.
He told me, afterwards, the damnèd spot
Was blood, his own. "Well, blood is dirt," I said.

"Blood's dirt," he laughed, looking away,
10 Far off to where his wound had bled
And almost merged for ever into clay.
"The world is washing out its stains," he said.
"It doesn't like our cheeks so red:
Young blood's its great objection.
15 But when we're duly white-washed, being dead,
The race will bear Field-Marshal God's inspection."

18 *Who Is Involved?*

The message in this poem is very powerful, but before we consider how Owen achieves this, we must try to discover who is involved in the scene and make some sense of the situation of the poem.

After first reading the poem in full, it might be apparent that there are several voices at the start in particular and a number of people are referred to throughout. We also see that Owen is using a lot of direct speech in the piece (just note the speech marks at the start of many of the lines). Therefore, our instincts should tell us that, in order to understand the poem better, we will have to read particularly carefully at these potentially confusing stages.

Let's begin by carefully examining the first stanza in our usual style. We must be aware of pronouns and full stops. Pronouns indicate who is involved and the full stops give us an indication of where the 'sentence sense' of the lines comes to an end:

> "**You**! What d'**you** mean by this?" **I** rapped.
> "**You** dare come on parade like this?"
> "Please, sir, it's –' "'Old **yer** mouth," the sergeant snapped.
> "I takes '**is** name, sir?" – "Please, and then dismiss."

We can explore the first line in isolation in this case at it is a single complete sentence:

> "**You**! What d'**you** mean by this?" **I** rapped.

Now, the first word is a second-person pronoun 'You' and this indicates a direct address – the sense that someone or some people are being spoken to directly. We see the pronoun used again immediately after ('What d'**you** mean by this?') and now we have to wait to learn if the pronoun 'you' is singular or plural – is one person being spoken to, or are a number of people being addressed? Also, at the end of the first line we have the first-person pronoun 'I' and therefore we have found our speaker. As we have seen before in Hardy's poem, 'The Voice', we have 'I' and 'You' pronoun combinations which give us a sense of one person talking directly to another. The grammar of the opening line also indicates that the direct speech '"You! What d'you mean by this?"' is spoken by the speaker, as is the second line: '"You dare come on parade like this?"' Here we have the 'You' pronoun used again as another direct address.

For example, if we were to write the first two lines in their 'sentence sense', they would read as if spoken by one voice (the speaker of the poem):

> **"You! What d'you mean by this?" I rapped. "You dare come on parade like this?"**

Reading on, the third line is quite a difficult one to work out:

> "Please, sir, it's –' "'Old yer mouth," the sergeant snapped.

In this line, we find that there are two voices: one is unspecified so we have to think logically about whose voice this is, and the second voice is a new voice in the poem and identified as belonging to 'the sergeant'. Let's look at the first part of the line closely: '"Please, sir, it's – "'. This is obviously a response to the first two lines (as spoken by the speaker), so we can safely assume that this is the 'You' figure who is being addressed *by* the speaker in the first line. We hear the voice of this person, but it is interrupted by the third figure in the poem: the sergeant.

We should pause here, just to clarify. Let's write down what we have discovered so far:

> **In Owen's poem 'Inspection' there are three figures – the speaker, the anonymous addressee, and the sergeant.**

By slowing down with our reading at this stage, we should then be able to picture a quite complex scene more clearly. This is good advice for anyone trying to get to grips with a difficult poem for the first time. Never rush the reading of a poem. Take the time necessary to question the details and to picture the scene clearly.

Moving on, the next line is another potentially confusing one as, once more, it includes two unidentified voices – so Owen is really making the reader do a lot of imaginative work here:

> "I takes **'is** name, sir?" – "Please, and then dismiss."

The first half of the line '"I takes 'is name, sir?"' is interesting as it is written colloquially and shows the speaker's accent and class. If written grammatically it would read, 'Shall I take his name, sir?' and, therefore, in the logical sequence of the conversation in the scene, this line is most likely said by the speaker as a question to his senior officer, the sergeant, who in turn responds with a response and final order: '"Please, and then dismiss"'.

Once more, with a poem that is so dense with **dialogue**, we should consider rewriting the lines (for our own sake) in order to get clearer sense of the sequence. Here is how the first stanza would read if it were written as **prose** in its 'sentence sense', giving a new paragraph whenever there is a new character speaking:

> **"You! What d'you mean by this?" I rapped. "You dare come on parade like this?"**
> **"Please, sir, it's –"**
> **"'Old yer mouth," the sergeant snapped.**
> **"I takes 'is name, sir?"**
> **"Please, and then dismiss."**

20   *Who Is Involved?*

To summarise at this stage, we can picture an opening scene involving three characters. The clues to the situation of the poem are there first in the title, 'Inspection', coupled with the fact that we have a 'parade' and a 'sergeant' in the scene. We can therefore picture a military inspection and assume that the speaker is some sort of officer (subservient to the sergeant) and that the anonymous 'you' figure of the poem is a lower-ranking soldier, a private, in all probability. Owen establishes the hierarchy between the three men quite starkly.

Such careful rereading at this early stage should now help us make sense of the rest of the poem. And, if we continue with our pronoun-hunting, we find that the tone of the poem shifts in the second stanza:

> 5   Some days 'confined to camp' **he** got,
>   For being 'dirty on parade'.
>   **He** told **me**, afterwards, the damnèd spot
>   Was blood, **his** own. "Well, blood is dirt," **I** said.

The third-person pronoun 'he' (line 8) is used by the speaker to describe the anonymous soldier of the opening stanza. We have a 'He' and 'me' pronoun pair on line 7, and a 'his' and 'I' pronoun pair on line 8 to indicate that in this middle phase of the poem Owen is concerned with the relationship between the speaker (the officer figure, as noted before) and this junior soldier (the anonymous 'he' of the poem).

In the final phase of the poem, very interestingly, there is an absence of the speaker entirely, and so the conclusion of the poem is devoted to the 'he' figure, the young soldier, of the poem:

>   "Blood's dirt," **he** laughed, looking away,
> 10 Far off to where **his** wound had bled
>   And almost merged for ever into clay.
>   "The world is washing out its stains," **he** said.
>   "It doesn't like our cheeks so red:
>   Young blood's its great objection.
> 15 But when we're duly white-washed, being dead,
>   The race will bear Field-Marshal God's inspection."

Owen uses direct speech again, and we are left to hear the final words of this soldier – the pronouns are seen in the phrases 'he laughed' (line 9) and 'his wound' (line 10) and 'he said' (line 12). At the end of the poem, it is evident, there is only one voice involved (the anonymous soldier), speaking directly to the speaker and – more importantly perhaps – to the reader.

There are some very interesting pronouns in the final five lines of the poem, so let's look at this passage in isolation:

> "**The world** is washing out **its** stains," **he** said.
> "**It** doesn't like **our** cheeks so red:

>   Young blood's **its** great objection.
> 15 But when **we**'re duly white-washed, being dead,
>   The race will bear Field-Marshal God's inspection."

Here, we have three related pronouns: 'its' used twice (on line 12 and line 14 respectively) and 'It' (line 13). All three refer to 'The world' as stated on line 12. 'The world' becomes the subject focus for the soldier's speech and we see it personified here (in a similar fashion to Hardy's **personification** of time and the passing century in 'The Darkling Thrush'). The world becomes a living entity (in the soldier's metaphor) which seems to be an enemy, fighting in opposition to the young soldiers.

We find this in the next important pronoun – a collective, plural pronoun: 'our'. Owen writes the lines:

> "**It** doesn't like **our** cheeks so red: / Young blood's **its** great objection."

The pronoun 'our' – as used by the anonymous soldier – therefore stands for all young soldiers who have signed up to war and who find that 'the world' (life, the war, the powers-that-be, essentially) is against the fighting men. Owen shows this collective suffering in the next important plural pronoun: 'we' as used on the penultimate line: 'when **we**'re duly white-washed, being dead' (line 15).

If we investigate the very end of the poem, a further figure is mentioned – a new entity appears: 'Field Marshal God'. This is a highly ironic way for Owen to close the poem. By introducing an all-powerful deity here, the hierarchy is complete. Of all the figures involved in the war, God is at the top, the sergeant is second, the speaker (the officer) is third, and the subject of the poem (the anonymous soldier) is last, along with all the other young soldiers who were drafted for war.

We might therefore see the importance of evaluating pronouns and other figures right to the end of the poem here, as the final entity – the ironic deity, 'Field Marshall God' – is at 'the heart' of the central theme of Owen's poem. If Owen's poem criticises the hierarchy of power in the army, and the fact that millions of young men were sent to their deaths in the fighting, it must be highlighted that the great commander 'God' looked on and continued to give those terrible orders, allowing such unnecessary deaths, too.

And by examining pronouns in this way, we have also, significantly, charted the development of the situation of the poem. We have seen that the poem starts with a military inspection and a scene in which a young soldier is being reprimanded on parade by both the officer and the sergeant. However, in the middle phase of the poem, the situation changes and Owen shows how an intimate relationship forms between the officer and soldier in their discussion about the blood ('the damnèd spot') on his uniform which got the soldier into trouble in the first place. As noted, the poem shifts then in the concluding phase, when Owen leaves us with the sole voice of the young soldier who remarks that the world is against them (him and his fellow soldiers) and that their enemy is not only the opposition forces but the world and the war itself.

22   *Who Is Involved?*

After all of this hard work, we are in a position to summarise this very complex poem clearly and confidently:

> **In Wilfred Owen's war poem, 'Inspection', the main subject of the scene is a young soldier who is being reprimanded for a dirty uniform whilst on parade. The speaker of the poem is a sympathetic officer who has to discipline the soldier, and through the interactions between the pair, we learn of the young soldier's criticism of war and a sense of his injustice at the blood that has been spilt in the fighting. It is clear that this criticism of war forms a central theme in Owen's poem throughout.**

Once more, we might consider how confidently and succinctly the poem is summarised here. We know what effort goes into this and it should be a great reward to think that we can get to grips with such difficult and complex poems in this fashion.

We have now summarised four quite difficult poems in a succinct style. Over time, the art of getting to 'the heart' of the poem becomes more instinctive and much quicker.

Practice, however, is key. Therefore, what we have next are two further poems – another by Thomas Hardy ('The Ruined Maid') and another by Wilfred Owen ('Disabled').

Practice

By using our new method, try to write a summary of each poem. Make sure your summaries are not overlong and absolutely no more than 100 words!

Here is a checklist of things to consider:

- Read the poem in full.
- Read the early parts of the poem carefully.
- Read through the lines to the full stops.
- Find and annotate the pronouns.
- Label the pronouns to make them clear.
- Identify the speaker of the poem.
- Look for clues to other voices, people, or figures involved.
- Look for clues to the situation and setting.
- Look for the 'sentence sense' of the lines in the poem – sometimes three or four lines (or even more) will make a single sentence.
- Try to establish a central theme or big idea in the poem.

At the end of this practice you will find summaries of the poems (with the word counts), with which you might compare your own attempts. Remember, there are no right or wrong summaries; however, a balance is needed between the comments on the speaker, comments on the other figures involved, comments on the situation of the poem, and suggestions about the central ideas or themes of the poem.

The Ruined Maid
by Thomas Hardy

"O 'Melia, my dear, this does everything crown!
Who could have supposed I should meet you in Town?
And whence such fair garments, such prosperi-ty?" —
"O didn't you know I'd been ruined?" said she.

5 — "You left us in tatters, without shoes or socks,
Tired of digging potatoes, and spudding up docks;
And now you've gay bracelets and bright feathers three!" —
"Yes: that's how we dress when we're ruined," said she.

— "At home in the barton you said 'thee' and 'thou',
10 And 'thik oon', and 'theäs oon', and 't'other'; but now
Your talking quite fits 'ee for high compa-ny!" —
"Some polish is gained with one's ruin," said she.

— "Your hands were like paws then, your face blue and bleak
But now I'm bewitched by your delicate cheek,
15 And your little gloves fit as on any la-dy!" —
"We never do work when we're ruined," said she.

— "You used to call home-life a hag-ridden dream,
And you'd sigh, and you'd sock; but at present you seem
To know not of megrims or melancho-ly!" —
20 "True. One's pretty lively when ruined," said she.

— "I wish I had feathers, a fine sweeping gown,
And a delicate face, and could strut about Town!" —
"My dear — a raw country girl, such as you be,
Cannot quite expect that. You ain't ruined," said she.

Disabled
by Wilfred Owen

He sat in a wheeled chair, waiting for dark,
And shivered in his ghastly suit of grey,

24   *Who Is Involved?*

    Legless, sewn short at elbow. Through the park
    Voices of boys rang saddening like a hymn,
5   Voices of play and pleasure after day,
    Till gathering sleep had mothered them from him.

    About this time Town used to swing so gay
    When glow-lamps budded in the light-blue trees,
    And girls glanced lovelier as the air grew dim,—
10 In the old times, before he threw away his knees.
    Now he will never feel again how slim
    Girls' waists are, or how warm their subtle hands,
    All of them touch him like some queer disease.

    There was an artist silly for his face,
15 For it was younger than his youth, last year.
    Now, he is old; his back will never brace;
    He's lost his colour very far from here,
    Poured it down shell-holes till the veins ran dry,
    And half his lifetime lapsed in the hot race
20 And leap of purple spurted from his thigh.

    One time he liked a blood-smear down his leg,
    After the matches carried shoulder-high.
    It was after football, when he'd drunk a peg,
    He thought he'd better join. He wonders why.
25 Someone had said he'd look a god in kilts.
    That's why; and maybe, too, to please his Meg,
    Aye, that was it, to please the giddy jilts,
    He asked to join. He didn't have to beg;
    Smiling they wrote his lie: aged nineteen years.
30 Germans he scarcely thought of, all their guilt,
    And Austria's, did not move him. And no fears
    Of Fear came yet. He thought of jewelled hilts
    For daggers in plaid socks; of smart salutes;
    And care of arms; and leave; and pay arrears;
35 Esprit de corps; and hints for young recruits.
    And soon, he was drafted out with drums and cheers.

    Some cheered him home, but not as crowds cheer Goal.
    Only a solemn man who brought him fruits
    Thanked him; and then inquired about his soul.

40 Now, he will spend a few sick years in institutes,
     And do what things the rules consider wise,
     And take whatever pity they may dole.
     Tonight he noticed how the women's eyes
     Passed from him to the strong men that were whole.
45 How cold and late it is! Why don't they come
     And put him into bed? Why don't they come?

Summaries:

'The Ruined Maid' by Thomas Hardy:

> **In Hardy's dramatic poem, 'The Ruined Maid', there are two figures involved: the unnamed speaker, who is a young country girl, and Amelia, the supposed 'ruined maid' of the title. Hardy's poem is made up of a dialogue between the two characters after they bump into each other in town. In this deeply ironic poem, we learn of the social stigma attached to being a 'ruined maid', with Hardy seeming to criticise small-minded rural attitudes and highlighting the fact that such societal labels at the time of his writing were not necessarily fair or justified. [95 words]**

'Disabled' by Wilfred Owen:

> **Wilfred Owen's 'Disabled' is a poem written in the third person, in which the speaker acts like a commentator of the scene. The subject of the poem is a victim of war – a disabled soldier, who is wheelchair-bound and sitting in his room waiting desperately for help from the nurses. As the poem develops, Owen shows us the memories of this soldier and we learn of the great contrast between the soldier's happy life before war and the desperate reality he now faces as a consequence of the fighting. [90 words]**

As we see here, both summaries are written to around 100 words. We sometimes find, particularly with longer poems, a desire to write much more.

However, the art of getting to 'the heart' of the poem essentially lies in how succinctly we can grasp what is going on in general.

Ultimately, what we need to practise is our ability to keep a strong grip on the entire poem at all times, regardless of its length, in the clearest way possible.

We find this even more so as we move on to the next chapter.

2 What Is the Situation?

Now that we have done some extensive work on answering the question: 'Who is involved?', we can focus on a more detailed study of the situation of the poem.

Often we find that the situation of a poem is a brief scene or an important 'moment in time'. Poetry, by nature, is brief and essentially captures these precise 'moments'. Poetry is also the art of economy with words, after all, and a poem, unless it is an epic, narrative tale, lives by a concentration of language and form.

Therefore, we can come prepared when meeting any new poem, knowing that the few lines we read will generally be trying to capture an important scene or moment in a condensed space on the page. And, it is our job, as general readers and students, to piece the clues together in order to picture the scene vividly.

We have to work *with* the poem and even complete the poet's work in our minds through our imaginations.

As seen in the previous studies, typically, the figures involved in the poem go hand in hand with the situation of the poem; we cannot really know one without the other. Therefore, we can accept that poetry is dramatic by nature; after all, it involves a speaker, voices, and often includes other people or characters. So, with this in mind, there is often a need for us to imagine a 'scene' taking place when reading a poem. Depending on the poem, sometimes this is easy, sometimes this is more challenging.

To simplify, we must first think of the clues which will help us to picture the situation or the scene. For example, we can start to annotate and make notes on any descriptions of the setting, the place and location, the time, the landscape, the number of people in the scene, the mood and atmosphere, and the movement of the poem itself (whether the location shifts and changes at different stages throughout).

Let's put this into practice now and consider a few poems as studies. Here is a poem by Ted Hughes (1930–1998), which utilises a very unique speaker and setting. It is entitled 'Hawk Roosting':

Hawk Roosting

by Ted Hughes

    I sit in the top of the wood, my eyes closed.
    Inaction, no falsifying dream
    Between my hooked head and hooked feet:
    Or in sleep rehearse perfect kills and eat.

5   The convenience of the high trees!
    The air's buoyancy and the sun's ray
    Are of advantage to me;
    And the earth's face upward for my inspection.

    My feet are locked upon the rough bark.
10 It took the whole of Creation
    To produce my foot, my each feather:
    Now I hold Creation in my foot

    Or fly up, and revolve it all slowly –
    I kill where I please because it is all mine.
15 There is no sophistry in my body:
    My manners are tearing off heads –

    The allotment of death.
    For the one path of my flight is direct
    Through the bones of the living.
20 No arguments assert my right:

    The sun is behind me.
    Nothing has changed since I began.
    My eye has permitted no change.
    I am going to keep things like this.

Before we start our detective work, looking for clues to the situation of the poem, let us first turn back to our usual method and spend some time on the pronouns and the speaker. We should be able to get a good sense of the speaker now and find that in this poem Hughes creates a very dominant first-person figure throughout. We might note the number of first-person pronouns which litter the poem: 'I', 'me', 'my', and 'mine', for example. And, it is important that we do not neglect this essential groundwork, because we must remember that the situation of the poem only becomes more clear once we have understood who the speaker is and who else is actually present in the scene.

28   *What Is the Situation?*

In this particular poem, 'Hawk Roosting', the title acts as an important framing device – without it, we, as general readers, might be slightly at a loss and potentially confused. Here, Hughes explains who the speaker of the poem is: it is the voice of a roosting (or resting) hawk. Therefore, through this **anthropomorphism** (the writer's act of giving human shape to an animal or non-human being), we have to imagine right from the start a very unique speaker of the poem – a **persona**: that of a talking, thinking bird of prey!

If we forget this, or lose sight of this in our minds, then we lose a sense of the unique scene that Hughes has created.

Now we can turn our attention more specifically to the situation of the poem, and in order to do this we should examine the earliest parts of the poem first (typically the opening stanzas). We do this because the poet, generally, will seek to establish the situation and setting of the poem at the earliest stage – just like in the popular novels that we read where the writer has a duty to give the reader a clear sense of character and setting in the opening pages or chapters in order to engage us and help us to follow along.

Here is the first stanza:

> I sit in the top of the wood, my eyes closed.
> Inaction, no falsifying dream
> Between my hooked head and hooked feet:
> Or in sleep rehearse perfect kills and eat.

Again, if we return to our usual method of trying to read to the full stops in order to break up the poem into its 'sentence sense' we find that this first stanza includes two full stops; one at the end of line 1 and another at the end of line 4. As the first stanza is neatly contained in this way, we can slow down and carefully examine what is happening.

Let's look closely. The first line is **end-stopped** (a single line that ends with a full stop and makes grammatical sense by itself):

> I **sit** in the top of the wood, my **eyes closed**.

The next 'sentence sense' is found in lines 2 to 4:

> **Inaction**, no falsifying **dream**
> Between my hooked head and hooked feet:
> Or in **sleep** rehearse perfect kills and eat.

In order to achieve a sense of the situation or the moment itself, we can note some of the words and phrases which indicate this: 'I sit', 'my eyes closed', 'inaction', 'dream', and 'sleep'. 'I sit' is a particularly important phrase, because it enables us to understand the '**time sense**' of the poem. The 'time sense' enables us to learn if the action of the poem is taking place in the past, the

What Is the Situation?   29

present, or the future. 'Sit' in this case is a present tense verb, so we know that the situation of the poem is taking place 'live' in the present moment. We must be alert to verb tenses, therefore, as another way of understanding the specific situation of the poem. For example, the tone and mood of the poem differs depending on the 'time sense' – just imagine the difference between the present, past, and future 'time sense' of these lines: '**I sit** in the top of the wood'; '**I sat** in the top of the wood', '**I will sit** in the top of the wood'. The situation of the poem and the characterisation of the hawk here depend on the fact that Hughes *chooses* to write in the present tense.

And so, after carefully grouping these associated words, images, and phrases to create the overall situation or moment of the poem, we find that a scene starts to emerge, and that what we have essentially is a mental picture of a roosting hawk, positioned in the high trees in the present moment in time, inactive, sleeping, and dreaming of 'perfect kills' (line 4). What we must try to do from here on is to keep the bird's position in our minds as we read, until we have any indication that the scene and situation is changing or developing.

The interesting thing about 'Hawk Roosting' is that, as we read the poem, we find that the situation does not really change – the entire poem is one speech given by one character (a **dramatic monologue**) which takes place from the same position – the 'high trees' (line 5) of the wood:

5   The convenience of the high trees!
     The air's buoyancy and the sun's ray
     Are of advantage to me;
     And the earth's face upward for my inspection.

Here in the second stanza the hawk is still in the happy, convenient position of the tree tops. We get a sense of its elevated position with the associated images of air and sun (both indicators of height) and we sense the hawk is looking down as the 'earth's face is upward' for it to gaze down at.

The clues to the hawk's fixed situation remain evident throughout the poem. The third stanza keeps us safely in place: the hawk is still 'locked upon the rough bark' (line 9) of the topmost tree branch:

     My feet are locked upon the rough bark.
10 It took the whole of Creation
     To produce my foot, my each feather:
     Now I hold Creation in my foot

The situation of the poem changes slightly in the following stanzas, stanzas 4 and 5; however, the hawk's elevated, sky-bound position is secure:

     Or fly up, and revolve it all slowly –
     I kill where I please because it is all mine.

15 There is no sophistry in my body:
My manners are tearing off heads –

The allotment of death.
For the one path of my flight is direct
Through the bones of the living.
20 No arguments assert my right:

There is the contemplation on the hawk's part to 'fly up' (line 13) and a further suggestion of the hawk, on the move, in flight: 'the one path of my flight is direct / Through the bones of the living' (lines 18 to 19). But, with careful reading we should be alerted to the important phrase 'Or fly up' on line 13. The word 'Or' is a conjunction and in this case offers an alternative (not a definite) action to the preceding line: 'Now I hold Creation in my foot'. The 'time sense' is clear in the adverb 'Now' and the present tense verb 'hold' – these words more forcefully imply that the hawk is still roosting on the tree branch rather than choosing to fly off and hunt.

Reading through the poem to the final stanza there is still a further sense of the 'inaction' (line 2) which is established in the beginning of the poem:

The sun is behind me.
Nothing has changed since I began.
My eye has permitted no change.
I am going to keep things like this.

We see how 'the sun is behind' (line 21) the roosting hawk, 'nothing has changed' (line 22) and, still from the highest point in the tall trees, the bird declares: 'I am going to keep things like this' (line 24).

Once more then, after this important and thorough detective work, we are in a good position to attempt a summary of the poem:

In Ted Hughes' 'Hawk Roosting', the speaker of the poem is a powerful hawk who is situated in the tall trees, roosting, and musing on its position in the world. The poem reads like a dramatic monologue as we hear the sole voice of this bird of prey, contemplating the hierarchy of the natural world and happily accepting its place at the top. The fixed setting of the hawk, perched in the highest tree-top throughout the poem, is symbolic of Hughes' central idea here.

Let's look at another poem now. 'Piano', by D. H. Lawrence (1885–1930) is a prime example of a poem which seems to capture a 'moment in time':

What Is the Situation? 31

Piano

by D. H. Lawrence

    Softly, in the dusk, a woman is singing to me;
    Taking me back down the vista of years, till I see
    A child sitting under the piano, in the boom of the tingling strings
    And pressing the small, poised feet of a mother who smiles as she sings.

5   In spite of myself, the insidious mastery of song
    Betrays me back, till the heart of me weeps to belong
    To the old Sunday evenings at home, with winter outside
    And hymns in the cosy parlour, the tinkling piano our guide.

    So now it is vain for the singer to burst into clamour
10 With the great black piano appassionato. The glamour
    Of childish days is upon me, my manhood is cast
    Down in the flood of remembrance, I weep like a child for the past.

After conducting an exploration of the pronouns and the figures involved in this poem, we can see that we have a first-person speaker ('I', 'me', and 'my' pronouns are present throughout the poem) and a female singer at the start of the poem ('a woman is singing' on line 1). This information is clearly communicated to the reader to establish the scene; however, the poem then seems to introduce two new figures in the following lines: a 'child' (line 3) who is 'sitting under the piano' and a 'mother' (line 4) who 'sings':

    Softly, in the dusk, a woman is singing to me;
    Taking me back down the vista of years, till I see
    A child sitting under the piano, in the boom of the tingling strings
    And pressing the small, poised feet of a mother who smiles as she sings.

Now, if we were to read this too quickly without more careful consideration, we could perhaps be led to picture a scene in which four figures were physically involved in the scene: a woman singing, the speaker listening, a child under the piano, and a mother at the piano too. This, however, is a false sense of the scene and takes us away from the real situation of the poem.

    We must think logically and look at the clues to the true situation of the poem. There are some obvious clues on line 2, for example. This is a very important line and should not be glossed. In order to achieve the 'sentence sense' of this line we should read through the lines to the full stop in the usual style. Here are the lines rewritten:

32 *What Is the Situation?*

> **Softly, in the dusk, a woman is singing to me, taking me back down the vista of years, till I see a child sitting under the piano, in the boom of the tingling strings and pressing the small, poised feet of a mother who smiles as she sings.**

If we examine the syntax (order of information) of this sentence, we find the true situation of the poem is revealed through the 'time sense' of the scene. We find the action of the poem takes place in the evening ('dusk'). Also, we find that the action takes place in the present moment in time – indicated by the present **continuous verb** 'is singing' – as the anonymous woman performs her song for the speaker of the poem. Continuous verbs suggest an action that is ongoing or unfinished and so the ongoing singing of the woman becomes central to the situation of the poem here. Coupled with this is the next continuous verb 'taking' which shows how the live voice of the woman is transporting the speaker 'back down the vista of years', or back through his own memory, in the moment of hearing her song.

This feeds into the very important, yet subtle, phrase: 'till I see'. 'See', as used here, is a present tense verb, so we know that at this stage in the poem, the speaker sees 'a child' in his imagination; he 'sees' (or 'imagines') his younger self as part of the journey back through the years of his life. We must try to keep in mind that all of this is brought about *because* of the woman's song and Lawrence shows us how the speaker's memory goes deeper to include not only a reimagining of himself as a boy, but also of his mother in his childhood.

So, if we were to attempt a summary of the poem at this early stage we might write something like:

> **In 'The Piano', the speaker of the poem is in the company of a woman who is singing to him at the piano before he starts to remember his childhood and the close relationship he shared with his own mother.**

If we maintain the sense of the fixed setting of the poem throughout (knowing that the moment of the poem takes place in the room in which the speaker, the singing woman, and the piano reside), we can then understand how the second stanza of the poem gives us a similar sense of the speaker being transported 'back' in his mind to the 'old Sundays', his 'home', the 'cosy parlour', and his mother when he was a boy:

5   In spite of myself, the insidious mastery of song
    Betrays me back, till the heart of me weeps to belong
    To the old Sunday evenings at home, with winter outside
    And hymns in the cosy parlour, the tinkling piano **our** guide.

As a result now, the plural pronoun 'our' on line 8 makes greater sense as referring to both of these imagined figures (the speaker's younger self and his mother) from the first stanza.

If we turn back to our original investigations and remind ourselves that at the start of the poem an unnamed woman 'is singing' to the speaker in the present moment of the poem, then in our imaginations this voice should still be singing as the speaker drifts off in his memories. This is the situation of the poem: the fact that the live, present voice of the singing woman results in his remembrance of his childhood. Lawrence helps us to keep this sense of the singing voice in our minds, therefore, as he returns to it explicitly in the final stanza, as the volume of this voice increases to 'burst into clamour' (line 9):

> So **now** it is vain for the singer to burst into clamour
> 10 With the great black piano appassionato. The glamour
> Of childish days **is** upon me, my manhood **is** cast
> Down in the flood of remembrance, **I weep** like a child for the past.

Here, we are trying to identify the words which provide us with a 'time sense' for the poem. Adverbs like 'now' in line 9 signal to the reader that we have returned to the present. The present tense verb 'is' (used twice in line 11) and the final image of the poem 'I weep like a child', which is also written in the present tense, bring a very immediate, live picture in our minds. The speaker cries, or is crying as the poem closes. The poet wants us, as readers, to leave the speaker in this state and have him remain that way in our minds, therefore.

At this stage in our reading, we are ready to attempt a full summary of the poem:

> **In the poem 'Piano' by D. H. Lawrence we witness a speaker overcome by the power of song and the music of the piano. Lawrence describes a single setting in which a woman sings and plays at the piano as the speaker is transported back to memories of his mother and his childhood. An irony of the poem appears to be the fact that, although happy in themselves, these memories force the speaker into realising the lost innocence he now feels as an adult. Time and memory are, therefore, central ideas for Lawrence here.**

Let's turn to another poem now and put our method into practice once more. Here is the poem 'London' by William Blake (1757–1827):

London

by William Blake

> I wander through each chartered street,
> Near where the chartered Thames does flow.

34   *What Is the Situation?*

>   And mark in every face I meet
>   Marks of weakness, marks of woe.
>
> 5   In every cry of every Man,
>   In every Infant's cry of fear,
>   In every voice, in every ban,
>   The mind-forged manacles I hear.
>
>   How the Chimney-sweeper's cry
> 10 Every blackening Church appals;
>   And the hapless Soldier's sigh
>   Runs in blood down Palace walls.
>
>   But most through midnight streets I hear
>   How the youthful Harlot's curse
> 15 Blasts the new-born Infant's tear,
>   And blights with plagues the Marriage hearse.

This is a vivid poem with a very precise setting it seems; but first, let's read again carefully and establish the role of the speaker and the other figures in the poem. It is evident from the opening line that we have an 'I' pronoun and therefore we see the poem through the eyes of this first-person speaker. The presence of the speaker and the 'I' pronoun is seen throughout the poem in the first, second, and final stanza, so we know that the speaker is active in the poem at these important stages.

When reading through the poem, we also find there are several different people involved besides the speaker. Blake first describes 'every face' (line 3) and 'every Man' (line 5) at the start of the poem, which are his metaphors for 'everybody' or every 'person' – essentially the collective population of London.

However, as the poet continues describing the different figures involved in the poem, they become less general and more specific it seems. For example, we turn from all children – 'every Infant' on line 6 – to the individual chimney-sweeper of line 9. We also read of the individual soldier (line 11), the 'youthful Harlot' (line 14), and the 'new born Infant' (line 15) at the end of the poem. We can say, therefore, that this poem includes a whole collection of different people of differing ages: men, women, and children.

Further to this, when we apply these ideas to the situation of the poem itself, things become even more revealing. First we have Blake's title, which acts as an important and stark 'frame' for the poem. He calls the poem 'London' so we have our setting already. To hear or read the word 'London' conjures up an immediate sense of place in a reader's mind in this way. However, because Blake chooses not to qualify the word with an adjective or any other sense of subjective description (he doesn't call the poem 'Fair London' or 'Industrial London', for example), this means that the London we first start to picture is

What Is the Situation? 35

the London of our own experience and imagination. The descriptions of this particular 'London' which follow in the content of the poem perhaps become more surprising or revealing to the general reader as a result.

In the opening stanza, Blake also gives us the 'time sense' of the poem and he continues to provide a more precise sense of location:

> I **wander** through each chartered **street**,
> Near where the chartered **Thames** does flow.
> And mark in every face I meet
> Marks of weakness, marks of woe.

Here our present tense verb ('wander') gives a sense of the speaker on the move in the present 'moment in time' of the poem. As readers, we must keep this picture in mind as we follow our strolling speaker through the streets of London. And, if we look more closely at the details, we can place our speaker in a very specific part of London: the heart of the city, as he walks the streets which flank the River Thames. These clues start to produce a vivid scene as we imagine now the lone speaker pacing through the great city, marking (or observing) all of his fellow Londoners (the 'every face' of line 3). So it is possible to see how an understanding of the speaker and the figures involved in the poem start to come together with the situation and setting to really bring the poem alive in our minds.

Now, if we refer back to the other figures that we discovered are involved in the poem (the men and women, the children, the chimney-sweep, the soldier, the harlot – or prostitute –, and her new-born baby) with the framework that we have established for the setting, we can start to understand what sort of picture of London Blake is really interested in painting.

Let us consider, for example, the journey Blake's speaker undertakes throughout the poem. In stanza 1, the speaker starts to walk by the Thames and he begins to see the signs of 'woe' (line 4) in the faces of everyone he passes by. The setting of the poem doesn't change in stanza 2 but the situation does:

> 5   In every cry of every Man,
> In every Infant's cry of fear,
> In every voice, in every ban,
> The mind-forged manacles I hear.

Here Blake brings in the sounds of the crying and suffering of every Londoner and, in particular, every child: 'In every Infant's cry of fear' (line 6).

Stanza 3 also signals a change in the scene as we navigate the heart of the city and 'wander' with the speaker past the churches and the 'Palace' itself:

>   How the Chimney-sweeper's cry
> 10 Every blackening Church appals;

36   What Is the Situation?

>   And the hapless Soldier's sigh
>   Runs in blood down Palace walls.

We might have Buckingham Palace in mind as the seat of the British monarchy here.

Interestingly, if we follow the scene into the final stanza, Blake chooses to bring his speaker's journey to an end, not in the fine, upper-class sphere of the city, but in the 'midnight streets' – the backstreets of London – where the prostitutes with their new-born babies are left to cry and curse:

>   But most through midnight streets I hear
>   How the youthful Harlot's curse
> 15 Blasts the new-born Infant's tear,
>   And blights with plagues the Marriage hearse.

We should note that Blake chooses to end importantly on two of the most vulnerable figures – a desperate prostitute and her illegitimate child. This perhaps indicates the poet's central concern or theme for the poem overall. And, what we might find when we summarise the situation of Blake's 'London', therefore, is that it is a poem which shows a specific interpretation of London at the time of the poet's writing and he chooses this concluding image for lasting effect.

After this close exploration of the poem, here is a possible summary:

> **William Blake's 'London' is a presentation of the industrial city as seen through the eyes of a first-person speaker. The action of the poem shows how the speaker walks the streets and observes the many people who are suffering collectively and individually. Blake describes some of the public institutions (like the country's military, church, and government) and subtly implies that these might be held responsible. Blake chooses to focus on the most vulnerable figures in society – the impoverished women and children of the city – and his poem, therefore, becomes a window into the city's poverty and society's neglect.**

If we get into the habit of summarising poems in this way: by charting how the situation of the poem is established; how the poem has a 'time sense' and captures a 'moment in time' or movement; or how the scene and the setting can change throughout, then we are much better placed to find 'the heart' of the poem each time.

To finish this section, let's look at a more modern, **free-verse** poem by the American poet Jean Toomer (1894–1967). This poem is a fine example of when the situation of the poem on the surface level is not in fact the situation at all, because the entire poem operates as an **extended metaphor** or a **conceit**.

Beehive

by Jean Toomer

> Within this black hive to-night
> There swarm a million bees;
> Bees passing in and out the moon,
> Bees escaping out the moon,
> 5   Bees returning through the moon,
> Silver bees intently buzzing,
> Silver honey dripping from the swarm of bees
> Earth is a waxen cell of the world comb,
> And I, a drone,
> 10 Lying on my back,
> Lipping honey,
> Getting drunk with that silver honey,
> Wish that I might fly out past the moon
> And curl forever in some far-off farmyard flower.

First, we find that the poem reads as one continuous verse, of irregular line length, some long and some short. What we must be alert to with free-verse poetry of this nature is the natural stresses (words or syllables which are heavily or more noticeably intoned when spoken aloud) and the timing of the dramatic short lines. Next, when reviewing Toomer's poem 'Beehive' we can look for our pronouns, for example, and find that we have a first-person speaker on line 9 of the poem – this, interestingly becomes a point of focus for us because it is also a dramatically short line of only four syllables, all monosyllabic words: 'And I, a drone'. And this image forms one of the central ideas in the poem as we will find out when we conduct a fuller study into the situation of the poem throughout.

But to begin at the beginning, as we have been practising, we should note first the title 'Beehive', which acts as a frame for the poem. Also we should try to understand who else is involved in the action of the poem. It is a first-person piece and the speaker is highlighted explicitly on line 9, (in a fitting 'bee' reference which likens himself to 'a drone') and also on line 13, so it would seem fair to us that the speaker becomes the point of focus only in the concluding phase of the poem. When reading for other pronouns or references to other figures in the poem, it appears that the lone speaker (the individual bee of the poem) is placed in counterpoint to 'the million bees' (line 2) at the start of the poem, which sets up an interesting situation for the poem overall.

Now, let's explore the situation of the poem closely. If we look for the first natural stopping point of the poem, it arrives at the end of the first two lines with the semi-colon:

> Within this black hive to-night
> There swarm a million bees;

38 *What Is the Situation?*

Here we have the 'time sense' ('to-night') and the setting, which is the 'black hive'. It might occur to us that the adjective 'black' is an interesting description, possibly suggesting the amount of bees which are living and operating in this particular hive at the same time – the exaggerated number 'million', further impresses this image in our minds. So Toomer is quick, it seems, to establish this particular beehive right from the start – of a hive at night swarming with a million bees. For some readers, this might already strike an unsettling note. We might be questioning if this is in fact a literal beehive, probably sensing that it is not. We should be alert to this feeling as we read the poem, knowing that we might be working with metaphorical, rather than literal, descriptions therefore.

As we read on, we can observe with this poem that it is written in one complete sentence. The only full stop in the piece arrives at the end of the last line, line 14. After the first two lines and the semi-colon, which forms a natural early stopping point, we should therefore try to understand the developing phases of the poem and sense how the situation might change from this point on. Let's look at the next possible phase in the poem:

>   Bees passing in and out the moon,
>   Bees escaping out the moon,
> 5 Bees returning through the moon,
>   Silver bees intently buzzing,
>   Silver honey dripping from the swarm of bees
>   Earth is a waxen cell of the world comb,

We see how Toomer now focuses on the swarm of bees entirely, repeating the subject 'Bees' at the start of lines 3, 4, and 5. The accompanying verbs are all continuous and dynamic: 'passing', 'escaping', and 'returning', to give a sense of the incessant activity of the bees as they pass under the moonlight. We can see in the repetition also of 'moon' at the ends of lines 3, 4, and 5, that Toomer places great focus on this night-time scene in particular. Now this might also strike us as odd, when we consider the fact that bees do not operate at nighttime, honey bees in fact sleep at night. Now, when is a bee not a bee? That is the question? What appears to be happening is that Toomer is more suggestively building his conceit (or extended metaphor) that the beehive being described in the poem is not actually a beehive, but rather an unsleeping city, and that the million bees are not actually bees, but people – the inhabitants at its centre. We see that this is confirmed as the images build to the 'Silver bees' and the 'Silver honey', where 'silver' now works in two ways. In the more literal, surface meaning of 'silver', in the night-time scene described here, we might picture the reflections of the moon on the bees' bodies; however, as we have found that the situation of the poem is working more convincingly on a metaphorical level, the 'silver' more evocatively now suggests money, in the fact that the people of the city are working constantly, 'dripping' with 'silver honey', in the bid to earn more and more. If we need further confirmation that the poem is working as an extended metaphor for a cosmopolitan city, and is not merely describing a literal beehive, it is delivered to us on the important line 8, where the speaker compares the human society to a hive in the explicit metaphor: 'Earth is a waxen cell of the world comb'.

If we look to explore how the situation of the poem develops into the final stages of the poem, we can begin with the change of focus on line 9 as discussed before. This is where the speaker of the poem becomes the central focus:

> And I, a drone,
> 10 Lying on my back,
> Lipping honey,
> Getting drunk with that silver honey,
> Wish that I might fly out past the moon
> And curl forever in some far-off farmyard flower.

And now that we have established the extended metaphor clearly in our minds, images like 'drone' and 'silver honey' take on new significance in our understanding of the situation of the poem and the speaker's tone and attitude. With the focus on the speaker now as the tired, wearied worker bee – the 'drone' who is pictured 'lying' flat on his 'back', 'drunk' on the intoxicating, addictive 'silver honey' – we get a greater sense of Toomer's central idea behind the poem. The bee-speaker here, because of the conceit, therefore does not feel like Ted Hughes' persona of the hawk in 'Hawk Roosting'. No, Toomer's speaker has always been human, artfully comparing modern life to a beehive and his own existence as a worker bee. 'Beehive' now becomes a commentary on urban life, humanity's need for survival in the modern world, and the role of money in our lives. The final couplet summarises this idea artfully as the speaker dreams of an escape from the frenetic hive, with the romantic desire to retreat to the rural landscape, and the peaceful haven of a 'farmyard flower'.

Now we are in a position to attempt a summary of the poem:

> **'Beehive' by Jean Toomer is an inventive poem commenting on the need for individual identity in frenetic, modern day, cosmopolitan environments. It works by imaginative conceit, comparing city life to a beehive, in which the speaker is a wearied worker bee, a 'drone' who seeks a romantic escape to a rural life far away from it all: from the monotonous existence, the late-night shifts, and the obsessive pursuit of want and need.**

40   *What Is the Situation?*

Practice

This is a good moment to practise now. Here are two poems, from poets we have met before: 'Bat', by D. H. Lawrence, and 'Nurse's Song', by William Blake.

Take some time now to read the poems, then try to summarise the poems in our usual style, writing brief commentaries of no more than 100 words.

In each case pay particular attention to the situation of the poem. I have provided a possible summary of each poem at the end of this section with which you can compare your own summaries.

Again, take confidence in knowing that there is no right or wrong way of summarising poems — your only aim should be to get to 'the heart' of the poem on your own terms.

Bat

by D. H. Lawrence

    At evening, sitting on this terrace,
    When the sun from the west, beyond Pisa, beyond the mountains of Carrara
    Departs, and the world is taken by surprise…

    When the tired flower of Florence is in gloom beneath the glowing
5   Brown hills surrounding…

    When under the arches of the Ponte Vecchio
    A green light enters against stream, flush from the west,
    Against the current of obscure Arno…

    Look up, and you see things flying
10 Between the day and the night;
    Swallows with spools of dark thread sewing the shadows together.

    A circle swoop, and a quick parabola under the bridge arches
    Where light pushes through;
    A sudden turning upon itself of a thing in the air.
15 A dip to the water.

    And you think:
    "The swallows are flying so late!"

    Swallows?

    Dark air-life looping
20 Yet missing the pure loop…

A twitch, a twitter, an elastic shudder in flight
And serrated wings against the sky,
Like a glove, a black glove thrown up at the light,
And falling back.

25 Never swallows!
Bats!
The swallows are gone.

At a wavering instant the swallows gave way to bats
By the Ponte Vecchio…
30 Changing guard.

Bats, and an uneasy creeping in one's scalp
As the bats swoop overhead!
Flying madly.

Pipistrello!
35 Black piper on an infinitesimal pipe.
Little lumps that fly in air and have voices indefinite, wildly vindictive;

Wings like bits of umbrella.

Bats!

Creatures that hang themselves up like an old rag, to sleep;
40 And disgustingly upside down.

Hanging upside down like rows of disgusting old rags
And grinning in their sleep.
Bats!

In China the bat is symbol for happiness.

45 Not for me!

Nurse's Song

by William Blake

When the voices of children are heard on the green,
And laughing is heard on the hill,
My heart is at rest within my breast,
And everything else is still.

42 *What Is the Situation?*

5   "Then come home, my children, the sun is gone down,
     And the dews of night arise;
     Come, come, leave off play, and let us away
     Till the morning appears in the skies."

     "No, no, let us play, for it is yet day,
10 And we cannot go to sleep;
     Besides, in the sky the little birds fly,
     And the hills are all covered with sheep."

     "Well, well, go and play till the light fades away,
     And then go home to bed."
15 The little ones leaped, and shouted, and laughed
     And all the hills echoèd.

Summaries:

'Bat' by D. H. Lawrence:

> **'Bat' by D. H. Lawrence is a fluid, free-verse poem which captures the lively voice of the excitable speaker. The poem has something of a holiday spirit about it as the speaker takes in the picturesque Italian scenery from a terrace view, in a seemingly romantic evening scene. However, the poem has an inventive structure as we learn of the speaker's surprise in the middle phase when he mistakes swallows for bats in the night sky, and his focus turns from his early whimsical thoughts to a highly detailed study of the disgusting bats themselves. [95 words]**

'Nurse's Song' by William Blake:

> **William Blake's poem, 'Nurse's Song' is a gentle and intimate scene, which describes a playful conversation between a nurse (the speaker of the poem) and the children she is employed to look after. Blake conjures up a picture of green parks and gardens in which the children play and laugh, while the Nurse looks and listens on from distance. Blake includes direct speech in the poem to give a dramatic quality throughout, showing the innocence and love in this particular adult–child relationship. [82 words]**

3 What Is the Central Theme?

The next part of our study is perhaps the most important. Trying to speculate on or determine the central theme of a poem is a difficult business for us as readers. For a start, we are dealing with a degree of speculation and imaginative thinking. We find that we need to go beyond the more concrete aspects of a poem, like the people involved and the setting, to commenting on the more abstract aspects, like the poet's intentions, the poet's concerns, or the poet's message for the readers, for example.

This is where the reading of poetry either excites or terrifies. Some readers enjoy the guesswork required and the imaginative-leaping necessary when trying to consider the big idea which drives the given poem and has motivated the poet to write it. On the other hand, some readers sometimes find that they are completely stumped when trying to answer questions about *why* the poet has written a particular poem in a particular way.

However, if we consider the previous steps which we have taken in trying to get to 'the heart' of the poem – often, by understanding the speaker, the other figures, and the situation of a poem – we find we can confidently assess the central theme or main idea of the poem accordingly. For example, you might have noted that in each of the summaries seen so far, there has always been a suggestion of a central theme emerging from the important details of the poem – from the figures involved and the situation.

As ever, making statements about the central theme in a poem takes a bit of practice. From experience we might find that a single poem has three or four possible themes driving it; however, with confidence, we can learn to make judgements in our commentary which might include one or two of these big ideas while rejecting others.

After all, on any given day, we might find that a poem offers up an idea or theme which we had not considered before, for example. Our response to the poem, thereafter, will change. Rather than this be a frightening thing, it should instead bring confidence.

We can take solace from the fact that a poem might *say* something to us one day and something else the next. As long as we are making judgements *from* the things we read – the things we find alive *inside* the poem and not outside it – our speculations on the themes of a poem will be both convincing and relevant.

DOI: 10.4324/9781003207511-4

44   *What Is the Central Theme?*

To simplify, when we are faced with the next poem, once we have established the speaker, the other figures involved, and the situation of the poem, we can start to evaluate the central theme by considering the following questions: Why has the poet written this poem? What is the possible message for the reader? Why has the poet written the poem like this? Why has the poet structured ideas in this way? Why has the poet started and ended the poem in this way?

What we can note here is that most of the questions start with 'Why has the poet...?' If we start to imagine answers to these questions ('Why? Why? Why?') when we read, we might find our understanding of the poet's craft and the poem itself become a lot deeper and more instinctive.

Let's start by looking at one of Shakespeare's sonnets. A **sonnet** is a particular type of poem, written with 14 lines. Shakespeare (1564–1616) wrote 154 of these. Here is 'Sonnet 2':

Sonnet 2

by William Shakespeare

> When forty winters shall besiege thy brow,
> And dig deep trenches in thy beauty's field,
> Thy youth's proud livery so gazed on now,
> Will be a tattered weed of small worth held:
> 5   Then being asked, where all thy beauty lies,
> Where all the treasure of thy lusty days;
> To say, within thine own deep sunken eyes,
> Were an all-eating shame, and thriftless praise.
> How much more praise deserved thy beauty's use,
> 10 If thou couldst answer "This fair child of mine
> Shall sum my count, and make my old excuse,"
> Proving his beauty by succession thine.
>   This were to be new made when thou art old,
>   And see thy blood warm when thou feel'st it cold.

Now, before we start to approach the central theme of this poem, let's return to our usual method and identify the speaker, the figures involved, and the situation of the poem.

By habit, when we reread the lines we should be on the lookout for pronouns, references to other figures or voices, the full stops in the poem (for the verse paragraphs or 'sentence sense'), and other clues to the situation, the 'time sense', and setting of the poem.

What we might need to note, when reading poems from the Renaissance period, is how poets like Shakespeare would use the now-antiquated, informal pronouns for 'you'. We see these in words like 'thou' and 'thee' (which are 'you' pronouns in the subject and object class of a sentence respectively) and 'thy' and

What Is the Central Theme? 45

'thine' (which are possessive pronouns, which mean 'your' and 'yours' respectively). It is a good idea to try to become familiar with these pronouns in order to understand the work of Shakespeare and his contemporaries better.

'Sonnet 2' is an interesting poem because it lacks any first-person pronouns to signify the first-person speaker directly – however, the voice of the sonnet still operates in the first person. The poem, we find, is a speech or monologue, spoken by one figure and the speaker of the poem, in this case, is addressing his speech to one specific person: the 'you' of the poem, as indicated by the host of second-person pronouns ('thy', 'thine', and 'thou') throughout. Essentially, the poem is made up of these two figures – the speaker, who is speaking the speech and addressing it to the listening addressee. With poems like this (and like many of Shakespeare's sonnets) this two-person scene forms the dramatic situation for the poem: of one person speaking directly to another.

In the final part of 'Sonnet 2', however, there is another figure mentioned: the 'fair child' of line 10. And, when reading carefully, the context of the poem shows that this child is actually the hypothetical son of the addressee (as imagined by the speaker). The pronoun, 'his' on line 12 also refers to the hypothetical child. This child is an interesting inclusion in the poem and our senses should be alert to this as we consider why Shakespeare includes this figure in the poem a bit later on.

But first, let's consider the early details of the poem. As we explore further, looking for the possible themes, our method remains the same. We should explore the first part of the poem and identify the first full stop so that we can deal with the 'sentence sense' of the poem. The first significant punctuation mark, we might argue, therefore, is the colon at the end of line 4. The first full stop is on line 8. However, eight lines written out as a single sentence might still be too complicated to understand clearly, so let's look at the 'sentence sense' of the first four lines and go from there:

> When forty winters shall besiege thy brow,
> And dig deep trenches in thy beauty's field,
> Thy youth's proud livery so gazed on now,
> Will be a tattered weed of small worth held:

Here are the lines, written out as a full 'sentence sense' with the antiquated pronouns changed into the modern 'you' form:

When forty winters shall besiege [your] brow and dig deep trenches in [your] beauty's field, [your] youth's proud livery (clothing) so gazed on now will be a tattered weed of small worth held.

If we are to paraphrase (put into our own words) here, we might find that the speaker's opening statement to the addressee is a warning of sorts. The speaker essentially states that when the addressee turns 40 years old and his face is full of wrinkles, the youthful beauty he currently has will become tattered and of little value.

The opening statement of the sonnet is, therefore, perhaps starting to address big ideas about time, ageing, and growing old. Conversely, some might argue that the big idea at this stage in the reading of the poem might be a warning about fading beauty. But, we must read on and see whether Shakespeare actually develops these themes throughout or introduces new ones instead.

Let's look at the next 'sentence sense' in the poem, line 5 to line 8:

5   Then being asked, where all thy beauty lies,
    Where all the treasure of thy lusty days;
    To say, within thine own deep sunken eyes,
    Were an all-eating shame, and thriftless praise.

Just to practise (this is a good habit with Shakespeare's language), we can write the lines again into a full sentence:

> **Then being asked where all [your] beauty lies, where all the treasure of [your] lusty (youthful) days, to say within [your] own deep sunken eyes were an all-eating shame and thriftless (pointless) praise.**

Here the speaker imagines the addressee's answer to the questions 'Where is your beauty?' and 'Where is the beauty you had in your youth?'. The speaker does not wait for an answer however, and mockingly speculates that the answer is already clear in the addressee's future, aged, 'deep sunken eyes' as a sign that the beauty is faded and lost.

We can look at this again in light of the opening four lines of the poem and perhaps state that the central theme of the poem is still focused on the big ideas of time, ageing, and fading beauty. Let's bear this in mind as we enter the concluding phase of the poem.

As we read on, we find that a third figure is involved in the poem – the 'fair child' on line 10 – so we might consider how this influences or affects the already established themes of the poem.

Lines 9 to 12 are perhaps the most complicated because the 'sentence sense' is written in the **conditional** or **hypothetical tense** (If you could…) and also includes some direct speech. Let's look carefully at these lines:

    How much more praise deserved thy beauty's use,
10 If thou couldst answer "This fair child of mine
    Shall sum my count, and make my old excuse,"
    Proving his beauty by succession thine.

If we rewrite the lines we get this:

> **How much more praise deserved [your] beauty's use, if [you] could answer: "This fair child of mine shall sum my count and make my old excuse," proving his beauty, by succession, [yours].**

In this part of the poem, the speaker therefore creates an imaginary situation in which the addressee has a child – a successor. The speaker imagines that the addressee's beauty can only be put to good use in this way: by having a 'fair child' that will inherit the speaker's beauty and keep this beauty alive 'by succession'. Now, because of this new idea, the theme of the poem seems to be developing further, into something more specific. We might ask now: Why does Shakespeare start to develop the poem along these lines and include this hypothetical child into the speaker's argument?

We could answer that the themes of time, growing old, and fading beauty are being developed now to include ideas of procreation and the future too.

With this in mind, the persuasive message of the speaker all hinges on the 'time sense' of the poem. If we evaluate this throughout the poem – the first 'time sense' is given in the opening line of the poem: 'When forty winters **shall** besiege thy brow'. What we have here is a **future tense**, so we know that the addressee is much younger than forty at the present moment of the speaker's speech. We know that in the present 'moment in time' of the poem the addressee's youth and beauty 'so gazed on **now** / **Will** become a tattered weed' (lines 3 to 4). The words in bold give us our 'time sense' – the **adverb** 'now' for the present of the poem and the **modal verb** 'Will' for the future.

And so, with this in mind, we might now be in a better position to understand the impact of all this on the concluding phase of the poem. It seems that Shakespeare's speaker heightens his warning to the addressee about the terrible visions of the future and growing old before he offers a hypothetical solution to the ageing problem: have children in order to preserve your beauty.

This is confirmed in the final **couplet** (the last two lines) of the poem. Here is the speaker's summary essentially of the entire poem and the final 'sentence sense':

> This were to be new made when thou art old,
> And see thy blood warm when thou feel'st it cold.

To simplify then, we can rewrite it, using what we have discovered already:

> **This (having a child) were to be new made when [you are] old and see [your] blood warm when [you feel] it cold.**

48   *What Is the Central Theme?*

We can see that the message from the speaker is clear in this summary statement — that by having a child, the addressee can live on (in theory) even after he is dead. Now, we must try to consider this in our summary of the poem. We have been able to see how Shakespeare establishes some general themes early on in the poem: ideas about time, growing old, ageing, and fading beauty, for example. But, he develops them as the poem goes on into something more specific. At the close of the poem we see, more importantly, further themes of procreation, mortality, life and death.

With all this information to hand, we should now try to make a confident decision and summarise the poem around some of these central themes. Here is an example:

> **Shakespeare's 'Sonnet 2' is a philosophical poem which discusses the important issues of time and growing old. In the poem we hear a persuasive speaker who seems to warn the youthful and beautiful addressee about the dangers of ageing. The speaker urges the addressee into preserving his life and beauty by having a child to carry on the line and it becomes apparent that the central theme of Shakespeare's poem is the human need for procreation and regeneration as the only practical way to overcome our own mortality.**

We are now in a position to look at another poem. For this study, we can try another sonnet (a 14-line poem), this time by the great, Romantic poet, William Wordsworth (1770–1850). The poem is entitled, 'Composed upon Westminster Bridge, September 3, 1802':

Composed upon Westminster Bridge, September 3, 1802

by William Wordsworth

    Earth has not any thing to show more fair:
    Dull would he be of soul who could pass by
    A sight so touching in its majesty:
    This City now doth, like a garment, wear
5   The beauty of the morning; silent, bare,
    Ships, towers, domes, theatres, and temples lie
    Open unto the fields, and to the sky;
    All bright and glittering in the smokeless air.
    Never did sun more beautifully steep
10 In his first splendour, valley, rock, or hill;
    Ne'er saw I, never felt, a calm so deep!

> The river glideth at his own sweet will:
> Dear God! the very houses seem asleep;
> And all that mighty heart is lying still!

Now, this is a very elegant **lyric poem**. Some readers might note the pleasant, detailed descriptions at 'the heart' of the poem. Other readers might note that there is not a great deal of action in the poem, nor are there any people or figures other than the speaker – a figure who plays something of a secondary role in the poem it seems. A poem like this then, with these sorts of patterns, might be considered a philosophical piece, a 'musing' by the poet, a consideration or observation of some important aspect of life and human existence. It is with poems like this that our focus on central themes and big ideas, rather than on people and the situation of the poem, really helps us get to 'the heart' of the poem.

However, let's start with our usual method first and consider the title, the speaker, the pronouns, and the situation of the poem. Let's look to break a poem like this into its 'sentence sense' by finding the verse paragraphs, the full stops, and by treating the poem in clear stages. As we do this, we should also try to consider what central themes or big ideas the poet is trying to establish. Remember, we can continue to ask the questions: Why has the poet done this? Why has the poet structured ideas in this way? Why has the poet started the poem and concluded the poem in this way?

Let's address the title of Wordsworth's sonnet first. In this instance, he does a lot of work for the reader and uses the title (like other poets we have encountered) as an important frame for the poem. He tells us, quite simply, the location and setting of the poem. His lines are 'composed' in London, specifically on Westminster Bridge in the heart of the great city. We also have September as a setting, and so, when reading, we might start to imagine a late summer scene as the backdrop for the piece.

Now let's look for the full stops. It seems the first full stop is on line 8; however, we should note Wordsworth's particular use of colons in this poem, as colons are strong punctuation marks which suggest a dramatic or significant pause between sentences. In this poem the colons work in a similar fashion to full stops, so we can also consider colons as making 'sentence sense' accordingly.

Here are the first eight lines of the poem. (interestingly, the first eight lines of a sonnet are typically called '**the octave**'.) This section of the poem is composed of two colons and one full stop and is essentially made up of three 'sentence senses':

> Earth has not any thing to show more fair:
> Dull would he be of soul who could pass by
> A sight so touching in its majesty:
> This City now doth, like a garment, wear
> 5 The beauty of the morning; silent, bare,

50   *What Is the Central Theme?*

> Ships, towers, domes, theatres, and temples lie
> Open unto the fields, and to the sky;
> All bright and glittering in the smokeless air.

We might note in these lines the absence of the speaker figure. We hear a voice, of course, but there are no indications of first-person pronouns ('I', 'me', 'mine', 'myself', for example). When this happens, it can suggest to us that the focus for the poet is not the 'self' of the speaker, but is perhaps some other subject matter. If we reread the opening of the poem carefully we find that Wordsworth uses the familiar technique of personification in assigning capital letters for non-human entities. Here he personifies the 'Earth' and the 'City'. So, already, it shows us the importance of the 'City' as a central 'figure' in the poem for the poet. With this in mind, we might start to think that the role or significance of the city – the urban environment – is going to become the central theme for the poem, possibly. Let's look at the 'sentence senses' and discuss further.

The very first line of the poem, for example, forms a 'sentence sense':

> Earth has not any thing to show more fair:

'Earth' here, through Wordsworth's act of personification, immediately becomes a figure or an entity which is on display for the speaker. We read this opening line as a statement of fact – that, in the poet's mind, Earth has nothing more fair to present to us, in other words. We might wonder, because of the comparison ('not any **thing** to show **more** fair') in this statement, that Wordsworth will specify what 'thing' is actually most fair in the poet's mind. However, he does not tell us immediately.

If we read the next 'sentence sense' in the poem (line 2 to line 3), we find that Wordsworth is still delaying the revelation of this 'thing' most fair:

> Dull would **he** be of soul who could pass by
> A sight so touching in **its** majesty:

In these lines, Wordsworth uses the universal pronoun 'he' to signify all of humanity. (We must remember that at the time of Wordsworth's writing, to use the masculine pronoun in this way was not a politically incorrect form of address.) These lines could therefore be rephrased as:

> **Dull would [a person] be of soul, who could pass by a sight so touching in its majesty.**

Wordsworth, therefore, still delays revealing this 'sight' which he deems the most fair. The ambiguous pronoun 'its' on line 3 continues this mystery. We might question why Wordsworth is delaying the revelation of the real subject of the poem for us. Does he want to create a dramatic revelation perhaps, by drawing out the suspense in this fashion, of the most beautiful thing on Earth?

In Wordsworth's poem we have to wait until line 4 and the next 'sentence sense' of the poem (line 4 to line 8):

> **This City** now doth, like a garment, wear
> 5 The beauty of the morning; silent, bare,
> Ships, towers, domes, theatres, and temples lie
> Open unto the fields, and to the sky;
> All bright and glittering in the smokeless air.

So we now know that it is 'this City' – the London of 1802 in the glorious 'morning' of September – that becomes the subject for the poem and the fairest 'thing' the Earth can 'show'. The situation of the poem is becoming clearer to us also. The focus of the poem is not on any one person or people – there is a distinct lack of people in the poem. What we find instead is that the poem is a contemplation by the speaker, standing upon Westminster Bridge, admiring the beauty of London. If we consider the precise situation of the poem, we have clues which tell us that the morning is 'silent' and 'bare' and the scene is seemingly perfect as all is 'bright and glittering in the smokeless air' (line 8). With this in mind, we might question what the reason for writing the poem in this way is. What themes are being introduced? It seems, then, that Wordsworth is creating an urban poem – a praise of the city in this romantic idealisation of London. If we evaluate the next stage of the poem, we can assess how this theme develops or changes.

The exclamation at the end of line 11 gives our next 'sentence sense':

> Never did sun more beautifully steep
> 10 In his first splendour, valley, rock, or hill;
> Ne'er saw I, never felt, a calm so deep!

We do find a change in the situation of the poem here. The speaker takes a stronger role in the concluding phases and it appears that the poet describes a series of natural elements in the poem ('valley, rock, or hill') – a rural aspect that goes in contrast to the urban theme established early on by the poet. The repetition of 'never' is worth noting here as it shows the rarity of the sight and experience as described by the speaker. The 'moment in time' of the poem is one of first and rare experience, of epiphany, therefore; of seeing the most beautiful city sunrise and feeling the deepest calm and serenity.

The poem closes with similar images of serenity:

> The river glideth at his own sweet will:
> Dear God! the very houses seem asleep;
> And all that mighty heart is lying still!

The river here is, of course, the River Thames which moves gently and 'glideth'. An interesting tone is built into the poem by Wordsworth. He uses exclamations to give an excited sense of voice to the speaker of the poem: 'Dear God!' shows the speaker's awe-struck response to the sleeping sense of the capital city ('the mighty heart' of London, to explain the metaphor), that September morning of 1802.

And so, if we evaluate our findings at this stage, we can observe that Wordsworth's concern in this poem seems to be in developing the central theme of the beauty of the city and in capturing the moment of observation – this sudden illumination. There is a developing idea in the second half of the poem that pitches the beauty of the city against the splendour of the natural world, concluding with the idea that it is the urban environment – the capital city – that is perhaps the most beautiful of all. With this in mind, let's attempt a summary of the poem:

> **In the sonnet, 'Upon Westminster Bridge, September 3, 1802,' William Wordsworth captures a late-summer morning in the city of London and describes its beauty. What we find as the poem develops is the central theme emerging: how it is possible for the man-made beauty of an industrial city to appear far more beautiful than the natural, rural world itself.**

So we see, when we explore the possible central themes in this way, our understanding of the given poem becomes deeper and this also enables us to evaluate more effectively. As ever, our aim is to try to get to 'the heart' of the poem and to 'grasp' it by summarising succinctly. And we find, by building our summary comments around a central theme, we can keep the entire poem in mind at all times far more easily.

As a way of consolidating our work now, let's look at a poem by Robert Browning (1812–1889), which makes explicit use of time markers and **temporal adverbs** for effect.

Home-Thoughts, from abroad

by Robert Browning

>   Oh, to be in England
>   Now that April's there,
>   And whoever wakes in England
>   Sees, some morning, unaware,
> 5   That the lowest boughs and the brushwood sheaf
>   Round the elm-tree bole are in tiny leaf,
>   While the chaffinch sings on the orchard bough
>   In England – now!

And after April, when May follows,
10　And the whitethroat builds, and all the swallows!
Hark, where my blossomed pear-tree in the hedge
Leans to the field and scatters on the clover
Blossoms and dewdrops – at the bent spray's edge –
That's the wise thrush; he sings each song twice over,
15　Lest you should think he never could recapture
The first fine careless rapture!
And though the fields look rough with hoary dew,
All will be gay when noontide wakes anew
The buttercups, the little children's dower
20　 – Far brighter than this gaudy melon-flower!

Before we look closely at some of the interesting time references in the poem, let's continue with our method first of all and search for the pronouns in the poem. When scanning for these, we can find that there are important 'my' and 'you' pronouns evident in the poem. The 'my' pronoun in the second stanza on line 11 indicates that we have a first-person speaker for the poem, and the 'you' pronoun on line 15 appears to be a universal address to the general reader, or listener, as the speaker passes comment on the 'wise thrush', the songbird, which is described at this stage in the poem. A closer observation of the pronouns supports the sense of general address to the reader in the 'whoever' reference on line 3 (here the speaker seems to be remarking on the people of England as a collective) and the 'he' pronouns on lines 14 and 15 refer to the thrush once more.

With this information in mind, we can make some confident statements about the poem. We know that when a first-person speaker speaks directly to an impersonal, universal addressee in this way, we have the basis for a lyric poem – in essence, a monologue or series of exclamatory contemplations from a sole voice, often confessional or revelatory in tone. Browning's poem does not employ an intimate, personal speaker–addressee situation as we might see in a Shakespearean sonnet for example (in which one figure speaks privately to a particular person); rather it aims at something more philosophical or generally contemplative, as we have already experienced with Wordsworth.

From this early information-gathering and initial groundwork, we can then turn to the title: 'Home-Thoughts, from abroad', and consider its impact in greater detail. With careful attention, we can see how important it becomes as a frame for the poem itself. 'From abroad', for example, immediately denotes the geographic position of the speaker at the present moment of the poem's action, and 'Home-Thoughts' already suggests a driving theme for the piece.

Even at this stage, when speculating on the central themes, we might start thinking that Browning's poem is concerned about big ideas of time and the changing seasons, and how the speaker's being in a certain location (a foreign land, far from home) inspires his strong feelings of patriotic longing.

54 What Is the Central Theme?

In turn, when we read the poem again deliberately, with the title as a frame, we see these ideas quickly develop:

>Oh, to be in England
>Now that April's there,
>And whoever wakes in England
>Sees, some morning, unaware,
>5   That the lowest boughs and the brushwood sheaf
>Round the elm-tree bole are in tiny leaf,
>While the chaffinch sings on the orchard bough
>In England – now!

As noted, the longing tone of the speaker is evident in the opening exclamation: 'Oh, to be in England'(line 1). By this, we know that the speaker must be located in some other country, far from his English home. And here is where we find Browning emphasising the situation of the poem – in this case, through exaggerated time references, in particular. Browning uses the repeated temporal adverb 'now' on lines 2 and 8 to draw our attention to the present moment of the poem, the sense of its being 'April', of spring. From here, the central themes for the poet start to emerge: of distance, of longing, of time, of place, and of seasonal change.

The verbs Browning uses are in the present tense too. The trees 'are in tiny leaf' (line 6) at the moment of the speaker's contemplations, and the songbird, the chaffinch, 'sings' (line 7). So overall, we find that the images of spring, of native bird life and budding plant life, are heightened because of Browning's emphasis on the 'now!' of the poem in the opening stanza. The vitally present moment, therefore, which the poet is keen to stress, exists in the very language he employs.

And so, as we read on, knowing that the speaker is far from England's shores at the present moment of the poem, the images of springtime in England which are created in the mind of the speaker take on new significance. We sense how a greater poignancy and feeling of longing is derived when we realise again that the speaker is only able to conjure up such romantic descriptions of the English landscape because of his remote position from his native home.

This is proof, once more, that if we, as readers, are constantly aware of the particular situation of the poem – the present moment itself – we can become sensitive, in this case, to the idea that Browning's speaker is having to create these images from memory because he is longing to return and not physically there.

We sense this further as we enter into the second stanza of the poem, and we receive a continuation of the speaker's fond and romanticised imaginings:

>And after April, when May follows,
>10   And the whitethroat builds, and all the swallows!

Hark, where my blossomed pear-tree in the hedge
Leans to the field and scatters on the clover
Blossoms and dewdrops – at the bent spray's edge –
That's the wise thrush; he sings each song twice over,
15 Lest you should think he never could recapture
The first fine careless rapture!
And though the fields look rough with hoary dew,
All will be gay when noontide wakes anew
The buttercups, the little children's dower
20 – Far brighter than this gaudy melon-flower!

Once more it is the time-markers, the verb tenses, and the temporal adverbs, which bring about the whimsical feeling and the distant longing of Browning's speaker.

We, as readers, are encouraged into following the series of contemplations by Browning's speaker as he takes us on an imaginative description through the months 'after April' (line 10) and into 'May' (line 10), as the migrant birds, the whitethroats, and the swallows, arrive in England and seek to build their nests. This stream of general observations becomes much more personal for the speaker as his imagination leads him to contemplate his own favourite tree: 'my blossomed pear-tree' (line 11). The possessive pronoun 'my' here takes us direct to the personal place of the speaker's memory, as if we are coursing across the landscape and then zooming in on this particular tree and this particular patch of land in England.

We should note the present tense verbs here and the nostalgic tone which really develops at this stage, as the speaker is reminded that life is ongoing in England in his absence – after all, his tree 'leans' and 'scatters' (line 11) its 'Blossoms and dewdrops' (line 13) while he speaks the lines of the poem, while another British songbird, the thrush, 'sings' (line 14) repeatedly and presently too.

However, as we follow the verb tenses carefully to the end of the poem, we can note a significant change in the tone. Good advice for any reader of poetry is to pay attention to the time shifts in the poem or to note when verb tense usage changes dramatically. In Browning's poem here, for example, we see the lasting sentiment of the poem changing, as Browning moves away from consistent present tense verbs to a future tense usage: 'All will be gay when noontide wakes anew / The buttercups' (lines 18 to 19). Here, the speaker, in praise of the English climate, knows that even though the fields of his homeland are 'rough' and frosty, and covered in 'hoary dew' (line 17) in the cold spring mornings, the little yellow buttercups of England's soil will still shine happily in the middle of the day. The speaker is convinced of the fact, it seems, because of Browning's well-timed shift in verb tense at the poem's close, from the lively present to the hopeful future tense, which provides a wonderful note of optimism for this nostalgic piece overall.

56 *What Is the Central Theme?*

As a last note on the tone of the poem, we should address the final line of 'Home-Thoughts, from abroad': 'far brighter than this gaudy melon-flower' (line 20). As we have seen, Browning's speaker has become full of nostalgia about England and has the image of the English buttercup fondly in mind as the poem concludes; this sets up the more bitter final line which includes a **comparative adjective**: 'brighter', to show that the speaker values the simple and symbolic beauty of the buttercup far more than the more exotic 'melon-flower' – the flower we imagine which is native to the foreign shores on which the speaker currently stands. This image is Browning's lasting attempt at securing the central theme of the poem through the situation and setting of the piece: that with foreign travel and physical distancing from our native lands, quite naturally, nostalgic longings and an awakened sense of patriotic pride arise.

In review then, we can see how, through skilful scene-setting and deliberate control of the time markers in the poem, a poet like Browning is able to conjure up a range of moods and feelings throughout. Accordingly, a number of central themes emerge from the situation of the poem itself if we are sensitive to verb tense shifts, temporal adverbs, and other associated imagery.

With all this in mind, we are now in a position to attempt a summary of Browning's poem:

> **Robert Browning's 'Home-Thoughts, from abroad' is a lyric poem with a great sense of nostalgia throughout. In the present moment of the poem the speaker is residing in a foreign country, far from his native England, and so we hear, as the poem develops through a series of deliberate time references, whimsical descriptions and lamenting exclamations, a great yearning for a return home. We see, as the poem concludes, Browning addressing a number of important associated themes – mainly those of patriotic pride, of memory and place, and of identity too.**

As we conclude this section, let's look at an inventive free-verse poem by Poet Laureate, Simon Armitage (1963–), called 'Zoom!':

Zoom!

by Simon Armitage

>   It begins as a house, an end terrace
> in this case
>   but it will not stop there. Soon it is
> an avenue

5   which cambers arrogantly past the Mechanics' Institute,
    turns left
        at the main road without even looking
    and quickly it is
        a town with all four major clearing banks,
10 a daily paper
        and a football team pushing for promotion.

    On it goes, oblivious of the Planning Acts,
    the green belts,
        and before we know it it is out of our hands:
15 city, nation,
        hemisphere, universe, hammering out in all directions
    until suddenly,
        mercifully, it is drawn aside through the eye
    of a black hole
20 and bulleted into a neighbouring galaxy, emerging
    smaller and smoother
        than a billiard ball but weighing more than Saturn.

    People stop me in the street, badger me
    in the check-out queue
25 and ask "What is this, this that is so small
    and so very smooth
        but whose mass is greater than the ringed planet?"
    It's just words
        I assure them. But they will not have it.

Now this is a very interesting poem which utilises the important, ambiguous pronoun 'it' for desired effect. Accordingly, we find that 'it' forms the subject for the poem throughout, and we also discover quite quickly that we, as readers, have to do a lot of imaginative work with the poem to get to grips with the subject matter more precisely as the piece unfolds.

If we return to our usual method and conduct a scan of the pronouns, as noted, we find that the beguiling 'it' pronoun dominates. However, we do find the explicit presence of the first-person speaker in the final stanza of the poem: the 'me' (line 23) and 'I' (line 29) pronouns are witnessed only in the concluding stanza.

Once more, we should consider why Armitage does this. Why does he leave out, for the most part, the overt voice of the speaker? We might answer that it seems as though the speaker is not actually the focus of the poem, therefore – that rather the predominating subject is this ambiguous, slippery 'it' instead.

58   *What Is the Central Theme?*

Well, in order to explore this idea further, we need to conduct a more precise reading and analysis of the poem.

Let's begin by considering the title carefully and by trying to break up the poem into parts and by working to the natural stopping points (the verse paragraphs or 'sentence sense') in the poem. Again, when scanning for these stopping points, we see each of the three stanzas is self-contained, and that each ends with a full stop. This plays into our hands as we will be in a better position to divide the poem into its beginning, middle, and end phases and to assess the first, second, and third stanzas accordingly.

To begin with the title, 'Zoom!', we see that the word 'zoom' does not occur in the body of the poem itself, so it is likely to form something of an important frame for the poem instead. The word 'Zoom!' is a dynamic exclamation, an **onomatopoeic** sound effect, we might think, suggesting speed and noise and launching or lifting off. Some of these notions might be relevant to us later on, so it is always worth considering the title in a bit of detail in this way.

Let's look closely at stanza 1 then, and try to understand the situation of the poem and the possible emerging central themes:

>   It begins as a house, an end terrace
>   in this case
>   but it will not stop there. Soon it is
>   an avenue
> 5   which cambers arrogantly past the Mechanics' Institute,
>   turns left
>   at the main road without even looking
>   and quickly it is
>   a town with all four major clearing banks,
> 10 a daily paper
>   and a football team pushing for promotion.

And as we start with our study of stanza 1, we can already see the title in action. The form of the poem, the free-verse style, with the long-short line dynamic and the frequent use of **enjambment**, give speed and momentum, right from the start, as the unnamed thing – the 'It' – of the opening line seems to grow and develop through the subsequent lines at tremendous speed. We can note Armitage's listing technique here and see how the nouns build: 'house' (line 1), becomes an 'avenue' (line 4) which becomes a prosperous and thriving 'town' (line 8). The speed of the arrival of these associated images in our mind, we could argue, comes back to the title – the zooming, unstopping sense of growth and development.

And now, we can step back for a moment and consider the central themes at play: are we already looking a poem whose central concern is progress and ideas of fast-moving change?

Let's read on and see if this becomes established in the next stanzas. Here is stanza 2:

> On it goes, oblivious of the Planning Acts,
> the green belts,
> and before we know it it is out of our hands:
> 15 city, nation,
> hemisphere, universe, hammering out in all directions
> until suddenly,
> mercifully, it is drawn aside through the eye
> of a black hole
> 20 and bulleted into a neighbouring galaxy, emerging
> smaller and smoother
> than a billiard ball but weighing more than Saturn.

So here we cans see the significance of Armitage's keeping the ambiguous 'it' unnamed. We get a sense of unending growth here, a spiralling out of control, as the little house at the start of the poem travels through the stages of progression: 'city, nation, / hemisphere, universe' (lines 15 to 16), until the whole thing implodes, seemingly to turn in on itself in the huge, stratospheric image of the 'black hole' (line 19), to become 'smaller and smoother', to be reduced to the size of a 'billiard ball' (line 22) at this turning point in the poem.

If we follow the situation of the poem so far, we find that we have read from the mundane starting point – the earth-bound non-descript 'house' of line 1 – to grow, expand, and travel out of the cosmos in the following twenty lines, to return dramatically to a point of prosaic smallness ('a billiard ball'). For Armitage, the unspecified, unnamed 'it' embodies a number of ideas: of rapid change, of impossible reach and development, of perspective and relative size, of peak and climax, of planetary bigness, of insignificant smallness.

Now, we might argue that all of these conflicting images confuse us, hindering us even from ever understanding the poem. However, this might be Armitage's point entirely. In short – he takes us to 'the heart' of the poem by making us consider something paradoxical, complex and unnameable.

The 'it' of the poem at this stage, however, is made of physical matter – we learn that it is solid, spherical, and weighty. The 'it' of the poem is perhaps suggestive of a planet in its own right, of a globe, or a sphere of mighty significance. We might be thinking that this entity could represent life itself, or more abstract notions like humanity or human nature? Once more, the art of this poem is that this goes undescribed by Armitage.

From here, we can evaluate this theme as we enter the final stanza:

> People stop me in the street, badger me
> in the check-out queue

25   and ask "What is this, this that is so small
   and so very smooth
      but whose mass is greater than the ringed planet?"
   It's just words
      I assure them. But they will not have it.

If we chart the situation of the poem (as it quite literally comes back down to earth), we see Armitage bring the scene to those mundane, everyday places: 'the street' (line 23) and 'the check-out queue' (line 24). And at last, in these anti-climactic, closing moments, Armitage finally reveals what the 'it' is to the reader.

Here, the physical presence of his first-person speaker is truly felt and the figure himself becomes something of a soothsayer, prophet, and poet as it appears that he is badgered by the average person on the street for answers to the philosophical question: 'What is this?'. And the answer which duly arrives is the weightiest matter, the most progressive, forward-moving, zooming, expanding, imploding, slippery entity of all: 'words', or 'just words' (line 28) to give it the bathetic quality so intended by Armitage.

This revelation arrives as something of a joke, but the timing of the delivery is something we should be alert to as this takes us to 'the heart' of the poem and the central themes. It appears to us that Armitage has managed to capture the nature of words and language in his playful use of pronouns, particularly the ambiguous 'it' pronoun, and the ironies and paradoxes he seems to pose so skilfully.

As ever, after such a discussion of the poem, we can make an attempt at a summary:

> **Simon Armitage's poem 'Zoom!' is the poet's playful attempt at capturing the essence of words and exploring the way language adapts and evolves. The free-verse form and the title 'Zoom!' help establish the speed of the poem as Armitage suggests throughout that words grow and take off at such extraordinary rate, while his inventive use of the ambiguous pronoun 'it' maintains the idea that language is ultimately slippery and that some nouns or objects are difficult to pin down or describe.**

Practice

Now is an opportunity to practise our summaries with a focus on central themes. Here are two poems: one by a poet we have met before, 'Sonnet 116' by Shakespeare; and one by a modern poet, Moniza Alvi, called 'An Unknown Girl', which employs the free-verse form to wonderful effect.

Remember to read the poems carefully a number of times, using the method of identifying the speaker, pronouns, other figures, the situation of the poem and, most importantly, the possible central themes in order to write succinct summaries of each poem. Try to write under 100 words in your summary writing.

At the end of this section, you will find two summary examples with which you might compare your own summary attempts. As ever, these are just a guide and not definitive summaries. Have confidence in your *own* readings and interpretations of the poems.

Sonnet 116

by William Shakespeare

    Let me not to the marriage of true minds
    Admit impediments. Love is not love
    Which alters when it alteration finds,
    Or bends with the remover to remove.
5 O no! it is an ever-fixed mark
    That looks on tempests and is never shaken;
    It is the star to every wandering bark,
    Whose worth's unknown, although his height be taken.
    Love's not Time's fool, though rosy lips and cheeks
10 Within his bending sickle's compass come;
    Love alters not with his brief hours and weeks,
    But bears it out even to the edge of doom.
    If this be error and upon me proved,
    I never writ, nor no man ever loved.

An Unknown Girl

by Moniza Alvi

    In the evening bazaar
    studded with neon
    an unknown girl
    is hennaing my hand.
5 She squeezes a wet brown line
    from a nozzle.
    She is icing my hand,
    Which she steadies with hers
    On her satin-peach knee.
10 In the evening bazaar

for a few rupees
an unknown girl
is hennaing my hand.
As a little air catches
my shadow-stitched kameez
15   a peacock spreads its lines
across my palm.
Colours leave the street
float up in balloons.
Dummies in shop-fronts
20   Tilt and stare
with their Western perms.
Banners for Miss India 1993,
for curtain cloth
And sofa cloth
25   canopy me.
I have new brown veins.
In the evening bazaar
very deftly
an unknown girl
30   is hennaing my hand.
I am clinging
to these firm peacock lines
like people who cling
to sides of a train.
35   Now the furious streets
are hushed.
I'll scrape off
the dry brown lines
before I sleep,
40   reveal soft as a snail trail
the amber bird beneath.
It will fade in a week.
When India appears and reappears
I'll lean across a country
45   with my hands outstretched
longing for the unknown girl
in the neon bazaar.

Summaries:

'Sonnet 116' by William Shakespeare:

> Shakespeare's 'Sonnet 116' is a carefully structured poem which essentially defines what true love is. The speaker is very persuasive in arguing throughout that a love of the mind is far stronger than any mortal, physical love. Shakespeare uses some big images in his poem, contemplating philosophical ideas of Love, Time, and Death in order to explain how a spiritual union between people can even live on eternally after we are dead. [71 words]

'An Unknown Girl' by Moniza Alvi:

> Moniza Alvi's free-verse poem, 'An Unknown Girl' captures the spirit of what it feels like to be a tourist or holidaymaker in an exotic foreign land. In the scene in the poem, the speaker embraces the culture of India, and we see her thoughts unravel as she receives a henna tattoo from the 'unknown girl' of the title. The short lines and the unique centring format provide speed and an excited tone throughout as the speaker comes to the realisation that this important event is something she will wish to remember long after the moment has passed. [97 words]

4 Practical Criticism and the 5-Part Essay

Now that we have spent some time practising how to read poems carefully and how to create succinct summaries of the poems that we encounter, we are in a very exciting position: we can begin to write more lengthy, critical poetry reports!

We can start to build on our initial summaries and conduct some more precise investigations of the given poem. A poetry report of this kind is called a 'Practical Criticism'. This is the surest test for any reader or English student as the report of the poem is without guideline – often we find that an essay question really helps us navigate our way through a poem in the classroom because we are able to read the poem with a certain focus throughout. However, the practical criticism report leaves it up to us simply to engage with the poem at hand and present our findings in as clear, detailed, and structured a way as possible.

Again, the freedom of practical criticism can delight and terrify students in equal measure.

What I hope to show in this section is how we can use the summary skills we have developed so far in the first three chapters as the perfect foundation for these types of poetry reports.

The art of practical criticism, after all, is in the structure of the essay. We must demonstrate an ability to keep the entire poem in mind throughout our writing whilst focusing at times on more precise parts of the poem too. This might seem like a difficult juggling act. However, if we simplify the structure of our essay, we can then be more elaborate and detailed in our commentary.

In order to do this we can work from a 5-part essay model. This is the most effective way of getting to 'the heart' of the poem.

The 5-Part Essay

The 5-part poetry essay follows this structure:

Part 1 – An Introduction
   In this part of the essay, we should seek to write a brief summary of the given poem and address some of the important general features, like

the role of the speaker, the other figures involved, the situation of the poem, and the possible central themes of the poem. Essentially, this part of the essay will read like the summaries we have practised in the previous chapters and should be written to around 100 words. It is vital that we establish a central theme at this stage because this will be our point of return throughout the rest of the essay. As we explore different aspects of the poem, we must repeatedly try to return to this central theme somehow – this is the key which provides structure to the essay.

Part 2 – *An Investigation of the 'Opening Phase' of the Poem*

In this part of the essay, we should seek to investigate how the poet starts the poem. We should comment on the *set-up* of the poem and quickly establish the role of the speaker and the other figures involved, along with our observations of the situation and setting of the poem. The comments we seek to make at this stage in the report should address the central theme that we established in our introduction.

Part 3 – *An Investigation of the 'Middle Phase' of the Poem*

In this important part of the essay, we are ultimately trying to explore how the poet *develops* the central theme and how the situation of the poem changes, is changing, or continues to build. We should try to identify turning points in terms of time and action; however, we must always bring our comments back to the central theme that we established in the introduction, in order for the essay to have a clear structure.

Part 4 – *An Investigation of the 'Closing Phase' of the Poem*

This is a vital stage in the essay, as we seek to demonstrate how the poet *concludes* the poem. We should examine the final images and lines of the poem and comment on their significance. Also, we must seek to comment on how the central theme extends into the final, concluding parts of the poem, and to what lasting effect.

Part 5 – *A Conclusion of our Investigation*

The conclusion to the essay gives us an important opportunity to reevaluate our findings and our thoughts on the poem as a whole once more. An important point to remember here in this section of the essay is that we do not simply repeat the introduction – this is a common error. No, in the conclusion we are now in a position to comment on the effectiveness of the poet's craft and technique. We can speculate on the writer's intentions here and also comment on how readers might respond to the poem. We must address the central theme in our conclusion, however, as this brings important structure to the overall report once more.

Well, the best way now to understand the 5-part 'Practical Criticism' essay is to read one and see it in action.

For practice, let's look at a sonnet – a 14-liner – by Christina Rossetti (1830–1894). The poem is entitled, 'Remember'.

Let's read it first, carefully!

Remember

by Christina Rossetti

> Remember me when I am gone away,
> Gone far away into the silent land;
> When you can no more hold me by the hand,
> Nor I half turn to go yet turning stay.
> 5 Remember me when no more day by day
> You tell me of our future that you planned:
> Only remember me; you understand
> It will be late to counsel then or pray.
> Yet if you should forget me for a while
> 10 And afterwards remember, do not grieve:
> For if the darkness and corruption leave
> A vestige of the thoughts that once I had,
> Better by far you should forget and smile
> Than that you should remember and be sad.

Now, here is a 5-part 'Practical Criticism' of 'Remember' by Christina Rossetti, with notes and observations accompanying each part of the essay itself.

Part 1 – An Introduction

In order to write an introduction, we must put our usual method into practice. After two or three careful readings of the poem, we can establish the key information: who is the speaker? Who else is involved? What is the situation of the poem? What are the possible central themes?

Here is a summary of the poem, written to no more than 100 words:

> **The poem 'Remember' by Christina Rossetti is a reflective sonnet, in which the speaker considers her own mortality and death. Rossetti describes a very intimate scene as the speaker addresses directly the loved one she is going to leave behind once she is dead. The poem is made up of the contrasting notions of remembering and forgetting, as the poet explores the act of grieving and what it means to accept death, for both the person dying and those left behind.**

What we should find in an effective summary like this is that a number of *key words* are used to define the poem. In this case, the key words are clear:

'reflective', 'mortality', 'death', 'intimate', 'contrasting notions', 'remembering', 'forgetting', and 'grieving'.

What we must try to do as the essay proceeds now is to continue returning to these key words throughout our writing. This, as mentioned before, will give us a clear and direct structure for the essay. Coupled with this, when reviewing the summary introduction, it is also important to establish a central theme as a 'point of return' throughout the writing.

And after reviewing the list of key words, for this essay, I have chosen to focus on **grief** and the act of **grieving** as the central theme.

Now, let's see how we can build from the introduction into a much closer exploration of the poem.

Part 2 – An Investigation of the 'Opening Phase' of the Poem

After reading the entire poem a number of times, it is important for us to try to make a judgement about the 'phases' of the poem. We should be in a good position to determine how the poet sets up and starts the poem and how the poet establishes the voice of the speaker, the other figures involved, the situation of the poem, and the central themes.

Now, however, we want to examine closely *how* the poem works in the opening phase.

If we continue with our usual method, we will find that by organising the poem into its 'sentence senses', we will be in a much better position to divide and section up the poem.

With Rossetti's sonnet, I have treated the first eight lines (also called the octave) as the opening phase of the poem:

> **Remember** me when I am gone away,
>   Gone far away into the silent land;
>   When you can no more hold me by the hand,
>   Nor I half turn to go yet turning stay.
> 5 **Remember** me when no more day by day
>   You tell me of our future that you planned:
>   Only **remember** me; you understand
>   It will be late to counsel then or pray.

What I noted in this section is Rossetti's focus on the title word 'remember' and how this forms the central idea in the opening of the poem. Also, we have two fullstops on line 4 and line 8; so the poem in the early phase is essentially composed of two 'sentence senses'.

I have also tried to keep the introduction summary in mind and also sought to refer to some of the key words from my introduction, bringing the central theme of 'grief' and 'grieving' into my discussion. These aspects will form the basis of my analysis.

Here is the next stage of the essay:

> **As the sonnet opens, Rossetti is quick to establish the intimate relationship between the speaker and the addressee. The poem becomes the private speech of one person to another. Here, the opening line of the poem is essentially a request by the speaker: 'Remember me when I am gone away' (line 1). From the beginning then, the speaker contemplates a life and a future in which she is absent and apart from the one she is leaving behind. The speaker repeats the emotive word, 'gone' in the second line to emphasise this idea of absence and parting, and it is only when she describes her future destination as 'the silent land' (line 2) that the theme of absence and parting becomes starker because this separation will be permanent as a result of her death. Here, Rossetti darkens the tone of the poem and we see notes of warning and regret in the speaker's words. The speaker admits her death will mean the addressee 'can no more hold' her 'by the hand' (line 3), for example. The intensity of the speaker's plea is seen in the repetition of the request 'Remember me' which appears on line 5 and again on line 7.**
>
> **Other interesting phrases which occur in the opening phase of the poem continue to develop the warning tone but also address ideas of the future that will be denied the speaker and the addressee. The negative phrase 'no more' reappears on line 5 as the speaker admits: 'no more day by day / You tell me of our future that you planned' (lines 5 to 6). Rossetti brings the urgency of the speaker to a climax at this stage in the poem, in lines 7 and 8. We find the refrain 'remember me' intensified with the adverb 'Only' on line 7: 'Only remember me', as the speaker confirms to the addressee on line 8 (if he did not know already) that once she is dead and gone it will be too late to do anything about it: 'It will be late to counsel then or pray' (line 8). We see in this dramatic opening to the poem how Rossetti demonstrates the difficulty of accepting the fact that our time is short, and that we are powerless to prevent death from separating us from our loved ones. What we also see here, is a natural longing on the speaker's part to want to be remembered and grieved for after she is dead.**

We should note that this commentary of the opening eight lines is written to around 400 words and is composed of two paragraphs. Because of the number of lines I have chosen to explore here (eight in total), there is consequently going to be more to write about (with other poems and other essays, the commentary for the opening might be shorter – there is no fixed rule!).

Essentially, we find that a commentary of this kind is based on various observations about the figures and themes in the poem and the patterns in the language (like repetition and changes in tone, for example). We can take confidence in the fact that it is not possible to comment on every line or every interesting moment in the poem. All we can do is make meaningful comments on the things *we* observe. There is nothing very technical or fancy in this type of writing; however, the comments and observations show development and progression, linking to each other as they build. This is essential in attempting to keep the entire poem in mind and in our grasp at all times, whilst building a convincing argument in our writing.

Part 3 – *An Investigation of the 'Middle Phase' of the Poem*

Now let's see how we can turn from our commentary of the opening phase into the middle phase. Remember, we are trying to consider how the poem develops or changes in terms of the speaker, the other figures, the situation, and the central themes.

After reading the poem a number of times, I have decided that lines 9 and 10 form the hinge or turning point for the poem. (In traditional sonnets, line 9 is often termed the '**volta**' or 'turn' in the poem – words like 'but', 'yet', and 'so', are commonly used at the start.) Also, the colon used at the end of line 10 gives a clear 'sentence sense' with which I can work clearly. My commentary for the middle phase of the poem is, therefore, going to be based around these two lines:

    Yet if you should forget me for a while
10   And afterwards remember, do not grieve:

Even though we only have two lines to explore here, it is possible to say quite a lot because it is important to keep the entire poem in mind at all times and to refer to some of the things we have mentioned before about the earlier phases of the poem in order to show a development and sense of structure in our commentary. A good practical criticism essay will show this and develop new points from those previously made.

Here are my observations about the middle phase:

> **However, as Rossetti develops the poem, we find that the tone of the speaker's words to the addressee changes dramatically. After the first eight lines, which included the repeated urge for the speaker to be remembered, the contrasting notion of 'forgetting' comes into play. We sense the tone in the speaker turn with the word 'Yet' at the**

> **beginning of line 9. It appears as if the speaker has reflected and considered that her repeated requests might have been too much. She says instead: 'Yet if you should forget me for a while / And afterwards remember, do not grieve' (lines 9 to 10). The new request and change of address arrives dramatically on line 10 therefore, in the short main clause: 'do not grieve'. Rossetti uses the caesura (the punctuation in the middle of the line) to dramatically slow the poem on line 10 in order to show that the speaker's thoughts have changed. The emotive word 'grieve' also becomes central to the poem as the speaker acknowledges that both remembering and forgetting are important parts of the grieving process. Here, quite selflessly she is prepared instead to be forgotten it seems by the addressee.**

The one thing I would highlight in this paragraph about the middle phase is the reference to **'caesura'**. This is a technical term which means a 'cut' in the line. This 'cut', break, or pause is formed by some form of punctuation – normally a full stop, a dash, a colon, or a semi-colon – to create a clear and dramatic pause in the middle of a line. However, commas can work effectively too. It is not essential for a student or general reader of poetry to know what a caesura is (we could equally comment on the fact that Rossetti's use of a comma on line 10 slows the poem down before dramatically revealing the main clause: 'do not grieve'); however, it is a useful term to know, if you want to use it, and sound more 'technical' in the future.

Part 4 – An Investigation of the 'Closing Phase' of the Poem

Now we can turn to the 'closing phase' of the poem. We are trying to develop the points we have already made as we seek to comment on the final images and lines of the poem. The final 'sentence sense' of Rossetti's sonnet is found in line 11 right through to the end of line 14:

> For if the darkness and corruption leave
>   A vestige of the thoughts that once I had,
> Better by far you should forget and smile
>   Than that you should remember and be sad.

Here are some observations on the closing phase of the poem:

> **As Rossetti brings the poem to its conclusion, the final four lines form the closing statement of the speaker's words to the addressee.**

> After the speaker's change of focus, from wishing to be remembered to wishing that the addressee does not grieve, the importance of 'forgetting' enters the poem. Images of 'darkness' (line 11) and 'corruption' (line 11) are acknowledged here, perhaps referring to the memories of the addressee's life and relationship with the speaker and 'of the thoughts that once' were 'had' (line 12) by the speaker. The final couplet of the poem becomes the speaker's lasting message to the addressee: 'Better by far you should forget and smile / Than that you should remember and be sad' (line 13 to 14). The contrast in these lines is most effective by the coupling of forgetting with happiness ('forget and smile') against remembering and misery ('remember and be sad'). In terms of Rossetti's attitude and understanding of the grieving process, she accepts here that it is in the difficult act of forgetting those we have loved that might bring the greatest comfort.

Part 5 – A Conclusion of our Investigation

After this examination of the 'Closing Phase' of the poem, we should attempt to wrap up the essay with a meaningful conclusion. We should read over our observations so far and note some of the patterns that have formed throughout.

We can consider the poet's craft (the way that the poet has 'made' the poem) and techniques, and also the poet's treatment of the central theme.

In a similar fashion to the introduction, we should try to make our conclusions relevant and succinct, rather than rambling and repetitive. We should also aim for around 100 to 150 words.

It is also advisable to clearly establish that the essay is coming to a conclusion by the standard phrases: 'In conclusion…'; 'In summary…'; 'To summarise…', for example.

Here is my attempt:

> In conclusion, Rossetti's sonnet, 'Remember' deals with the difficult concept of death and grief. Her poem gives some guidance, through the speaker's words to the addressee, about the correct way to grieve. As the words are spoken by the one who is dying or perhaps going to die first, the message in the poem makes a powerful claim that in the grieving process there needs to be a balance between remembering the deceased and forgetting them, in order for those left behind to get on with their own lives, to eventually 'smile' and recover over time.

Perhaps this is a good opportunity to read the practical criticism essay of 'Remember' in full now, without the interrupting notes. Try to get a sense of the structure of the argument and the development of the commentary as the essay builds to the conclusion. Here is the essay:

> **The poem 'Remember' by Christina Rossetti is a reflective sonnet, in which the speaker considers her own mortality and death. Rossetti describes a very intimate scene as the speaker addresses directly the loved one she is going to leave behind once she is dead. The poem is made up of the contrasting notions of remembering and forgetting, as the poet explores the act of grieving and what it means to accept death, for both the person dying and those left behind.**
>
> As the sonnet opens, Rossetti is quick to establish the intimate relationship between the speaker and the addressee. The poem becomes the private speech of one person to another. Here, the opening line of the poem is essentially a request by the speaker: 'Remember me when I am gone away' (line 1). From the beginning then, the speaker contemplates a life and a future in which she is absent and apart from the one she is leaving behind. The speaker repeats the emotive word, 'gone' in the second line to emphasise this idea of absence and parting, and it is only when she describes her future destination as 'the silent land' (line 2) that the theme of absence and parting becomes starker because this separation will be permanent as a result of her death. Here, Rossetti darkens the tone of the poem and we see notes of warning and regret in the speaker's words. The speaker admits her death will mean the addressee 'can no more hold' her 'by the hand' (line 3), for example. The intensity of the speaker's plea is seen in the repetition of the request 'Remember me' which appears on line 5 and again on line 7.
>
> Other interesting phrases which occur in the opening phase of the poem continue to develop the warning tone but also address ideas of the future that will be denied the speaker and the addressee. The negative phrase 'no more' reappears on line 5 as the speaker admits: 'no more day by day / You tell me of our future that you planned' (lines 5 to 6). Rossetti brings the urgency of the speaker to a climax at this stage in the poem, in lines 7 and 8. We find the refrain 'remember me' intensified with the adverb 'Only' on line 7: 'Only remember me', as the speaker confirms to the addressee on line 8 (if he did not know already) that once she is dead and gone it will be too late to

do anything about it: 'It will be late to counsel then or pray' (line 8). We see in this dramatic opening to the poem how Rossetti demonstrates the difficulty of accepting the fact that our time is short, and that we are powerless to prevent death from separating us from our loved ones. What we also see here, is a natural longing on the speaker's part to want to be remembered and grieved for after she is dead.

However, as Rossetti develops the poem, we find that the tone of the speaker's words to the addressee changes dramatically. After the first eight lines, which included the repeated urge for the speaker to be remembered, the contrasting notion of 'forgetting' comes into play. We sense the tone in the speaker turn with the word 'Yet' at the beginning of line 9. It appears as if the speaker has reflected and considered that her repeated requests might have been too much. She says instead: 'Yet if you should forget me for a while / And afterwards remember, do not grieve' (lines 9 to 10). The new request and change of address arrives dramatically on line 10 therefore, in the short main clause: 'do not grieve'. Rossetti uses the caesura (the punctuation in the middle of the line) to dramatically slow the poem on line 10 in order to show that the speaker's thoughts have changed. The emotive word 'grieve' also becomes central to the poem as the speaker acknowledges that both remembering and forgetting are important parts of the grieving process. Here, quite selflessly she is prepared instead to be forgotten it seems by the addressee.

As Rossetti brings the poem to its conclusion, the final four lines form the closing statement of the speaker's words to the addressee. After the speaker's change of focus, from wishing to be remembered to wishing that the addressee does not grieve, the importance of 'forgetting' enters the poem. Images of 'darkness' (line 11) and 'corruption' (line 11) are acknowledged here, perhaps referring to the memories of the addressee's life and relationship with the speaker, 'of the thoughts that once' were 'had' (line 12) by the speaker. The final couplet of the poem becomes the speaker's lasting message to the addressee: 'Better by far you should forget and smile / Than that you should remember and be sad' (line 13 to 14). The contrast in these lines is most effective by the coupling of forgetting with happiness ('forget and smile') against remembering and misery ('remember and be sad'). In terms of Rossetti's attitude and understanding of the grieving process, she accepts here that it is in the difficult act of forgetting those we have loved that might bring the greatest comfort.

> In conclusion, Rossetti's sonnet, 'Remember' deals with the difficult concept of death and grief. Her poem gives some guidance, through the speaker's words to the addressee, about the correct way to grieve. As the words are spoken by the one who is dying or perhaps going to die first, the message in the poem makes a powerful claim that in the grieving process there needs to be a balance between remembering the deceased and forgetting them, in order for those left behind to get on with their own lives, to eventually 'smile', and recover over time.

Some important notes about the style of the essay can be made:

- The 5-part essay does not mean the answer is written in five paragraphs. Sometimes we find that a particular phase of the poem needs more attention. In this case I needed two paragraphs for my observations on the opening phase of the poem.
- A range of quotations from the poem helps to support the points and observations made throughout.
- It is helpful to provide line references in brackets after quotations. This enables anyone reading the essay to follow along clearly and it enables us to check that we are making observations from all phases of the poem and that we are not just focused on one particular area of the poem throughout the essay.
- It is not possible to write about every aspect of the poem or every line, so we must pick and choose the lines, ideas, or moments in the poem that are relevant and meaningful for us and the discussion at hand.
- In each paragraph the central theme of 'grief' or 'grieving' is mentioned and this is important as it provides a clear structure for the essay. It is a good habit to get into. When we make our general observations about the poem we must be sure to bring them back to the central theme.
- The essay includes a range of detailed observations about the language and imagery of the poem, the tone, the role of the speaker, the situation, and setting – there is much to praise here because the observations are all worthy and naturally come out of the poem itself.
- The essay, therefore, does not need to be overly technical or fancy to be worthy of merit. For example, we haven't really addressed issues of form, meter, rhythm, rhyme, or sound effects, but this has not prevented us from understanding or getting to 'the heart' of the poem in convincing detail.

5 Three Essays

At this stage, it is important for us to become more familiar with the 'Practical Criticism' style. The best way to do this is simply to read more essays of this nature.

The following pages will explore three poems: 'Adlestrop' by Edward Thomas (1878–1917), 'Down by the Salley Gardens' by W. B. Yeats (1865–1939), and 'Wedding' by the modern English poet Alice Oswald (1966–) with accompanying essays.

Before reading the essays, however, it is good practice to first read the poems and spend five to ten minutes making your own notes and observations. Perhaps some of these observations will come up in the model essays that follow.

Adlestrop

by Edward Thomas

>   Yes. I remember Adlestrop—
>   The name, because one afternoon
>   Of heat the express-train drew up there
>   Unwontedly. It was late June.
>
> 5 The steam hissed. Someone cleared his throat.
>   No one left and no one came
>   On the bare platform. What I saw
>   Was Adlestrop—only the name
>
>   And willows, willow-herb, and grass,
> 10 And meadowsweet, and haycocks dry,
>   No whit less still and lonely fair
>   Than the high cloudlets in the sky.
>
>   And for that minute a blackbird sang
>   Close by, and round him, mistier,

15   Farther and farther, all the birds
      Of Oxfordshire and Gloucestershire.

> Edward Thomas's poem 'Adlestrop' is a quiet, reflective piece, which describes a solitary moment in the speaker's life. The speaker finds himself alone at Adlestrop train station and we find how time seems to slow as the speaker takes in the natural surroundings. Thomas brings in some gentle descriptions of nature and ends the poem contrastingly with an array of sound in the form of uproarious birdsong. A central theme for the poet seems to be the importance of human solitude in these moments of epiphany.
>
> The opening stanza of the poem immediately gives us a sense of the speaker who appears to be looking back or recounting this enlightening moment at Adlestrop. The voice of the poem sounds like someone remembering clearly to themselves: 'Yes. I remember Adlestrop—' (line 1). The dash here creates a deliberate pause as if the speaker is thinking carefully. Thomas uses the opening stanza of the poem to create a clear setting and situation. The event of the memory takes place in 'late June' (line 4) and we are left to picture the heat of the day and the 'afternoon / Of heat' (lines 2 to 3). We find that the memory is particularly clear for the speaker as something unexpected happens: 'the express train drew up' at Adlestrop Station 'Unwontedly' (line 4). Thomas uses enjambment here (in the run-on line) to emphasise the adverb ('Unwontedly') and to stress the fact that this memorable event was perhaps out of the ordinary, yet ultimately fated or meant to be. Here we get a sense that the epiphany which occurs later in the poem was also always meant to happen for the speaker.
>
> After this careful set-up to the poem, Thomas uses the middle stanzas to develop the feeling of solitude and isolation on the part of the speaker. The poet continues to slow the speed of the poem down with a deliberate caesura on line 5: 'The steam hissed. Someone cleared his throat' and there is a sense of expectancy here as we wait to find out whether this anonymous 'someone' will become central to the poem. However, the repetition in the following line: 'No one left and no one came' (line 6) emphasises the absence of people, action, and movement – a theme which is qualified by Thomas's image of the 'bare platform' (line 7).
>
> An interesting technique that Thomas uses is the enjambment again; however, in this instance he uses it to run stanza 2 into

stanza 3 as the speaker describes a list of observations, starting with the station's man-made sign and the name 'Adlestrop' which begins to merge with the wildflowers and the fields which are visible all around: 'willows, willow-herb and grass, / And meadowsweet, and haycocks dry' (lines 9 to 10). To continue the images of solitude and the lack of movement in the scene, the speaker compares these observations as being 'no whit less still and lonely fair' (line 11) than the 'cloudlets in the sky' (line 12). So, we have a scene of calmness, inaction, and tranquillity on this hot summer's day. The interesting oxymoron 'lonely fair' essentially summarises the mood of the poem: that loneliness and solitude are the most appealing things in such a moment.

The final stanza of the poem forms the contrasting moment of action against all of the preceding inaction. Here Thomas creates the epiphanic moment for the speaker as amidst all the solitude and seeming stillness, the speaker suddenly – as if for the first time – hears the great chorus of birdsong. Thomas creates a climax in the final stanza, which is essentially one complete sentence, to build momentum to the final line. Once more, it is the enjambment which brings momentum to the poem and creates the excitement of the final line. The speaker first notes the sole voice of the 'blackbird' (line 13) who is soon surrounded by other voices. Thomas shows by repetition and through the comparative adjectives 'mistier' and 'farther and farther', the great distance in the sound and range of the accompanying birdsong. As the poem builds to the final line, Thomas's memorable exaggeration that 'all the birds / Of Oxfordshire and Gloucestershire' (lines 15 to 16) can suddenly be heard by the speaker to gives a thrilling, excited tone to what has been a calm and sedate piece overall.

In conclusion, we find that it is through the great contrast in the action of the poem that Thomas is able to create the powerful impact of this moment of epiphany and realisation for the solitary speaker. It is through careful and deliberate scene-setting by Thomas and through his emphasis on humanity's relationship with the natural world that the final stanza has such weight of feeling. We also find that by the poet creating a speaker who is calm and deeply reflective, the excited reaction to and deep realisation of the latent beauty of nature upon hearing the great chorus of birdsong on this fated day is magnified too.

Some important notes at this stage in our study:

- Again, the 5-part essay does not necessarily mean five paragraphs. Here, the middle phase of the poem demanded more attention and so I needed two paragraphs to do this part of the poem justice.
- Perhaps this essay is starting to address more technical aspects of the poem, exploring, new terms like **caesura** (the 'cut' or punctuated line); **enjambment** (the run-on line when one line carries on into the next); **oxymoron** (a figure of speech which uses obvious contrast to highlight a feeling or effect).
- When writing a quotation which includes two lines, we must indicate the turn into the second line with a forward-slash (/). For example, this is seen in the quotation: 'willows, willow-herb and grass, / And meadowsweet, and haycocks dry' (lines 9 to 10).
- When we begin to notice the speed or pace of particular lines or passages in the poem, we are starting to address (in a very general way) issues of rhythm. This is a good habit to develop at this stage, because if we can attune our ear to the speed or pace of the poem, we will be able to address more technical ideas of rhythm and meter later on.

Down By the Salley Gardens

by W. B. Yeats

Down by the salley gardens
  my love and I did meet;
She passed the salley gardens
  with little snow-white feet.
5 She bid me take love easy,
   as the leaves grow on the tree;
But I, being young and foolish,
  with her would not agree.

In a field by the river
10 my love and I did stand,
And on my leaning shoulder
  she laid her snow-white hand.
She bid me take life easy,
  as the grass grows on the weirs;
15 But I was young and foolish,
  and now am full of tears.

The poem, 'Down By the Salley Gardens' by W. B. Yeats is a love song of sorts which describes the relationship between a young,

naïve speaker and his lover. The setting of the salley gardens is classically romantic; however, the relationship between the two figures in the poem is strained. Yeats manages to create feelings of pity and regret throughout this melancholic piece particularly through the power dynamic between the couple, which becomes a central focus for the poem.

In the opening stanza of the poem, Yeats introduces the salley gardens as the intimate meeting place of the couple – the speaker and the speaker's 'love' (line 2). The mood of the poem is established through the short lines and the song-like rhyme. In the opening lines we have the gentle rhymes – 'meet' (line 2) and 'feet' (line 4) – to create a sense of formal discretion in the couple's relationship and to highlight the grace of the unnamed woman. This elegance is also qualified in the adjective 'little' and in the purity of her 'snow-white feet' in line 4. The sound quality in these opening lines also suggests a hushed, softness to her movement, particularly in the sibilance (repeated 's' sounds) which exist throughout line 3: 'She passed the salley gardens'. It appears that the speaker is perhaps idealising the grace and elegance of this woman – his 'love' – in a classically romantic way and the dynamic between the pair is seemingly traditional in that of the relationship between a doting and infatuated lover and the object of his affection.

An interesting shift, however, occurs in this early stage of the poem, as the mood of the poem becomes slightly darker in lines 5 to 8. The revealing line is line 5: 'She bid me take love easy', and the emotive word 'bid' here suggests a reluctance on the lover's part to take such a strong part in this relationship. The verb even suggests a pleading on her part in the need to fend off the speaker's ardent love. It is difficult to establish where the power lies in the dynamic of their relationship at this stage in the poem, as it appears that each party holds a different perspective. In Yeats's description, the woman believes that love should be 'easy' and the simile 'as leaves grow on the tree' (line 6), considers a love that is at once both natural, alive in the spring and summer months, yet likely to fade in the winter season. It is a subtle comparison, but perhaps a realistic one on her part. We find that it is only through the speaker's retrospective tone – of looking back and reflecting on this advice – that he deems himself 'young and foolish'(line 7) for not having agreed 'with her' (line 8) on this view of their love.

The sense of distance and conflict that is subtly built into the opening stanza is the focus of the final stanza and conclusion to the poem. The setting seems to change – it is not entirely clear if these are the salley gardens are not – but Yeats brings the action of the poem to a non-descript field by the river. The indefinite article, 'a', in the phrase 'In a field' (line 9) suggests a less important, less emotionally significant place on the part of the speaker; accordingly, we see that the following image of the couple is very revealing. The rhyme in these lines of the poem 'stand' (line 10) and 'hand' (line 12) furthers the colder, more awkward body language between them and the overall platonic nature of their relationship: 'On my leaning shoulder / she laid her snow-white hand' (lines 11 to 12). In terms of the dynamic between them, this image is suggestive of her maternal stance in relation to him, of her gentle way of rejecting the speaker's love. Yeats's repetition of 'snow-white' (line 12) is poignant here, as it reiterates the beauty of the woman – a beauty that the speaker ultimately misses out on.

In the final four lines of the poem, Yeats skillfully sets up the refrain: 'she bid me take…'. However, here, rather than use the word 'love' (line 3), he replaces this with the word 'life' (line 13). Now the message from the woman to the speaker is clear: 'take life easy' – that she hopes he has a happy, stress-free future, a future full of love and romance, perhaps. The irony here is that it will be a future without her. Once more this is qualified by a natural simile – 'as the grass grows on the weirs' (line 14). However, this image has a greater sense of permanence, and this therefore suggests the woman wishes the speaker well. Here, Yeats manages to create a kindly, well-mannered figure of her and, as a result, magnifies the speaker's reckless youth and foolishness at not heeding her advice before. Yeats closes the poem with the speaker's confession – the refrain: 'But I being young and foolish' (line 15), before ending the poem on a desperate image of the mournful speaker, miserable and 'full of tears' (line 16).

In summary, Yeats presents quite a complex picture of this strained relationship. He uses song-like rhythms and rhyme to create a gentle pace to the poem, but, all the while, he pitches this against the image of a once-romantic relationship that has turned sour. This unsettling feeling permeates the poem ultimately and this is seen most clearly in the overall dynamic of the relationship between the central couple. We are perhaps left feeling little pity for

> the 'young and foolish' speaker and instead are left in praise of the worldly-wise and sensible woman. This is perhaps Yeats's sincere evocation of what young, inexperienced love feels like and the pain that comes with it.

Here are some further notes on the essay:

- With a seemingly shorter poem, there is a lot of potential for rich commentary. Just because a poem is short it does not mean that there is little to observe or say.
- In terms of being slightly more technical, this essay begins to comment on the sound quality of the poem and effects like **rhyme** and **sibilance** (repeated 's' sounds throughout a line).
- When commenting on rhyme it is advisable to choose one or two notable examples, to quote specifically the rhyming words, and to comment on the effect of these words. (We should only comment on these things, however, if they add to the essay itself and if they are important when trying to get to 'the heart' of the poem.)
- When commenting on sound effects like sibilance, we must consider the effect of the 's' sounds in a given line and speculate on what this sound adds to the poem. Typically, when dealing with 's' sounds we should consider the 'hard' or 'soft' quality of the sound. For example, in this poem, Yeats's use of sibilance is soft ('She passed the salley gardens') to evoke a sense of the woman's grace.
- We can sometimes be more precise when commenting on imagery and images in the poem. We can address **similes** (comparisons using the words 'like' or 'as', as seen in this poem: 'She bid me take love easy / As the leaves grow on the trees') in this way.

Wedding

by Alice Oswald

> From time to time our love is like a sail
> and when the sail begins to alternate
> from tack to tack, it's like a swallowtail
> and when the swallow flies it's like a coat;
> 5   and if the coat is yours, it has a tear
> like a wide mouth and when the mouth begins
> to draw the wind, it's like a trumpeter
> and when the trumpet blows, it blows like millions…

and this, my love, when millions come and go
10   beyond the need of us, is like a trick;
and when the trick begins, it's like a toe
tip-toeing on a rope, which is like luck;
and when the luck begins, it's like a wedding,
which is like love, which is like everything.

Alice Oswald's sonnet 'Wedding' is a celebratory verse, which carefully interweaves and harmonises a series of associated images, (some romantic, others ordinary and everyday) in order to consider what the nature of love is. The whole poem works as a single sentence, linking clause upon clause with deliberate repetition and fluid enjambment to bring about a feeling of the speaker's unravelling description of the personal love shared with the addressee.

Even though it is a modern composition, we can treat Oswald's sonnet in the way we would a traditional Shakespearean sonnet, as she essentially employs the three quatrain and final couplet division seen in Shakespeare's famous form. However, Oswald creates a slight tension in her poem by the rhyme scheme and inventive end-words, interchanging between moments of full rhyme ('sail' and 'tail' on lines 1 and 3), half rhyme ('alternate' and 'coat' on lines 2 and 4), consonantal rhyme ('trick' and 'luck' on lines 10 and 12), and feminine endings ('wedding' and 'everything' on lines 13 and 14), for example. This tension is evident in the first four lines of 'Wedding' where we find Oswald's ability to be suggestive, rather than assertive, establishes the overall mood and tone of the poem. We feel this right from the start in the opening phrase of the poem: 'From time to time...' (line 1). It is not a declarative 'Always...' or an assertion: 'Our love is...'; instead it is an adverbial phrase, suggesting an occasional love, which is followed by a series of comparisons by simile, which never seems to be able to define what love is exactly. For example, the shared love as declared in the opening line ('Our love') of the speaker and addressee is first likened to 'a sail' but it quickly becomes something else: a bird, 'a swallowtail', and then 'a coat', thus proving the point that in four lines and three similes the definition of love is still undetermined and unfixed. Oswald's rapid changing is suggestive of the abstractness of love, that it can have an essence

of all three concrete things: an alternating ship's sail, an adaptive, ever-moving swallowtail in flight, and an enshrouding coat – yet, it is also not entirely these things; it is something else, itself, undefinable.

This technique of frequent, looping repetition, (or anadiplosis, to use the rhetorical term) is effective at developing this sense of the shifting nature of love for the poet in the middle phase of the poem. The comparison of love with a coat in line 4, feeds into line 5, and becomes a more specific comparison – love for the speaker is a coat with 'a tear' – something imperfect perhaps. More precisely, Oswald uses the conditional tense for the first time here: 'and if the coat is yours' (line 5), to give the impression that the speaker is considering the personal relationship shared with the addressee in particular – not a general, universal love. The metaphor of the torn coat that represents their relationship is somewhat negative it seems; however, this is quickly remedied by the free-wheeling associations that follow. How quickly, with the fast-paced enjambment, does the tear in the coat become a provocative 'wide mouth' (line 6), which becomes a triumphant inhaler of the 'wind' (line 7) and then a loud 'trumpeter' (line 7) blowing a declaration for the world to hear. This is spiralling, energetic writing which comes back to earth with the surprising next simile: 'like millions' (line 8). We are left to question: Millions of what? Millions of other loves, possibly. Millions of other people who have loved before? In a clever contrast, the singular, personal love shared by the speaker and addressee, perhaps realistically, is compared to the loves that are shared by all those other lovers, easily getting lost and literally fading with the underwhelming thought. The poet's effective use of ellipsis (like millions...), creates this feeling, before the poem concludes with the final six lines to follow.

And, as the poem turns into its closing moments, on line 9, Oswald creates a volta, an important tonal shift in the poem. Here the speaker intimately addresses the one to whom they are speaking as 'my love' (line 9). The thought of the 'millions that come and go' (line 9), the masses that live around and 'beyond the need' (line 10) of the couple (the speaker and the addressee) is key in the conclusion of the poem. As we have seen, the sentiments in the first eight lines (the octave) were high-spirited, excitable, and playful, yet the series of similes seemed to fade on an exhausted thought, on an ellipsis – on a prosaic realisation. Here, however,

> in the closing sestet (technically the last six lines) of the poem, the gesture is heightened once again. The speaker isolates the couple's love from the rest of the common crowd, and it feels like 'a trick' (line 10), which becomes a daring act or a magic show – which becomes quickly like 'a toe / tip-toeing on a rope' (lines 11 to 12). This tentative tipping point of the enjambment on line 11, falling into line 12, and the delicate, clipped 't' alliteration here, bring about this sense of risk and chance, to feed into Oswald's next simile: that this sort of love is like 'luck' (line 12) – again, a very modern understanding, that with all human relations, a lot of the successes rely on a bit of good fortune: a sentiment which rejects more classical and romanticised ideas of love from the literary past. The final couplet of the poem is Oswald's brilliant harmonising of the similes throughout the poem – in the last two lines, with 'luck', love becomes 'like a wedding' (line 13) – a civil act of harmony – and a wedding by paradox becomes 'like love' (line 14), which in the mind of a modern poet like Oswald, then becomes not 'everything' (that might be too romantic-a-notion) but, 'like everything' (line 14).
>
> In conclusion, 'Wedding' reads as a valiant attempt on the speaker's part, through the many similes, to describe the abstract idea of love. But this is the charm of the poem and the sincere sentiment behind the writing: it is, after all, a love sonnet which is full of uncertainty and vulnerability. For Oswald, 'Wedding' appears as a deliberately backward way of coming to terms with love. An expression of love ultimately by a speaker who, ironically it seems, is happy to become exposed as not really knowing what love is.

Here are some further notes on the essay:

- Here, we explore the impact of form and consider how the traditional Shakespearean sonnet is treated by a modern poet.
- In terms of being slightly more technical, this essay begins to comment on the particular tone of the poem which is developed, in this case, by the series of similes throughout.
- Also, the nature of comparison by simile is discussed in some sophisticated detail, particularly as we address the great range of these comparisons and the overall effect that they produce, as desired by the poet.
- The comments on rhyme are also more precise, particularly when discussing how half-rhyme and consonantal rhyme create tension.

- The style of the essay is quite discursive throughout (perhaps moving away slightly from the more basic style of the Thomas essay on 'Adlestrop'), and poses questions and seeks to answer. It is therefore lively and engaging in tone – with practice and growing confidence, this style will become more natural and achievable.

Practice

Now is a fitting time to practise. On the following pages you will find three 'unseen' poems by poets we have met before: 'No, Thank You, John' by Christina Rossetti; 'Tears' by Edward Thomas; and 'The Lake Isle of Innisfree' by W. B. Yeats.

No, Thank You, John

by Christina Rossetti

    I never said I loved you, John:
        Why will you tease me, day by day,
    And wax a weariness to think upon
        With always 'do' and 'pray'?

5   You know I never loved you, John;
        No fault of mine made me your toast:
    Why will you haunt me with a face as wan
        As shows an hour-old ghost?

    I dare say Meg or Moll would take
10   Pity upon you, if you'd ask:
    And pray don't remain single for my sake
        Who can't perform that task.

    I have no heart?—Perhaps I have not;
        But then you're mad to take offence
15   That I don't give you what I have not got:
        Use your common sense.

    Let bygones be bygones:
        Don't call me false, who owed not to be true:
    I'd rather answer 'No' to fifty Johns
20   Than answer 'Yes' to you.

    Let's mar our pleasant days no more,
        Song-birds of passage, days of youth:

Catch at to-day, forget the days before:
   I'll wink at your untruth.

25 Let us strike hands as hearty friends;
      No more, no less: and friendship's good:
   Only don't keep in view ulterior ends,
      And points not understood

   In open treaty. Rise above
30   Quibbles and shuffling off and on:
   Here's friendship for you if you like; but love,—
      No, thank you, John.

Tears

By Edward Thomas

   It seems I have no tears left. They should have fallen—
   Their ghosts, if tears have ghosts, did fall—that day
   When twenty hounds streamed by me, not yet combed out
   But still all equals in their rage of gladness
5 Upon the scent, made one, like a great dragon
   In Blooming Meadow that bends towards the sun
   And once bore hops: and on that other day
   When I stepped out from the double-shadowed Tower
   Into an April morning, stirring and sweet
10 And warm. Strange solitude was there and silence.
   A mightier charm than any in the Tower
   Possessed the courtyard. They were changing guard,
   Soldiers in line, young English countrymen,
   Fair-haired and ruddy, in white tunics. Drums
15 And fifes were playing "The British Grenadiers."
   The men, the music piercing that solitude
   And silence, told me truths I had not dreamed,
   And have forgotten since their beauty passed.

The Lake Isle of Innisfree

By W. B. Yeats

   I will arise and go now, and go to Innisfree,
   And a small cabin build there, of clay and wattles made;
   Nine bean-rows will I have there, a hive for the honey-bee,
   And live alone in the bee-loud glade.

5   And I shall have some peace there, for peace comes dropping slow,
     Dropping from the veils of the morning to where the cricket sings;
     There midnight's all a glimmer, and noon a purple glow,
     And evening full of the linnet's wings.

     I will arise and go now, for always night and day
10 I hear lake water lapping with low sounds by the shore;
     While I stand on the roadway, or on the pavements grey,
     I hear it in the deep heart's core.

6 Answering an Essay Question

Now, we are in a position to move on from the traditional practical criticism essays and look at something more typical of a modern examination style question. Often, in an examination situation an unseen poem will be printed alongside a specific question, which asks the student to explore a particular area of the poem and to answer accordingly.

This, in many ways, is often an easier task than the practical criticism.

For example, the examiner might ask us how the writer 'presents' a particular idea or treats a particular theme in the given poem. Our job then is to read the poem through the 'lens' of the question and to provide only relevant commentary which applies to said question.

Let's look at an example:

How does Edna St Vincent Millay (1892–1950) present <u>strong emotions</u> throughout the poem, 'Time does not bring relief'?

Time does not bring relief

by Edna St Vincent Millay

    Time does not bring relief; you all have lied
    Who told me time would ease me of my pain!
    I miss him in the weeping of the rain;
    I want him at the shrinking of the tide;
5   The old snows melt from every mountain-side,
    And last year's leaves are smoke in every lane;
    But last year's bitter loving must remain
    Heaped on my heart, and my old thoughts abide.
    There are a hundred places where I fear
10 To go,—so with his memory they brim.
    And entering with relief some quiet place
    Where never fell his foot or shone his face
    I say, "There is no memory of him here!"
    And so stand stricken, so remembering him.

Well, this is a very good question, which gives us a clear focus area: 'strong emotions'.

So, the best approach to our answer will be to read the poem carefully again, and then to summarise some of the key ideas which relate somehow to strong emotions.

We want to maintain a good structure for our answer, so we return to the 5-part essay model and know that we can build the body of our response around the opening, middle and closing phases of the poem.

After this reading, it is evident that the poem is a sonnet (it has 14 lines) and it is constructed in three parts, like so: the opening phase of the poem is the first four lines, lines 1–4; the middle phase of the poem is lines 5–8; the closing of the poem is lines 9–14.

It would be helpful to have some sort of idea as to why the opening, middle, and closing phases are constructed in this way, so another good approach here is to label the three sections of the poem accordingly. To do this, we must keep the question in mind: 'strong emotions'. In general, we ask: How does the opening of the poem demonstrate or deal with strong emotions? How is this different from the emotions seen in the middle phase? How are these strong emotions revealed in the closing phase of the poem?

When reading the poem closely again, it appears that the overall tone is one of bitterness in the opening of the poem, heard most obviously in the voice of the speaker, and the first four lines which form the speaker's opening address. We learn quickly of the speaker's personal loss at the death of a loved one, and her anger at the people who have lied to her about the grieving process:

> Time does not bring relief; you all have lied
> Who told me time would ease me of my pain!
> I miss him in the weeping of the rain;
> I want him at the shrinking of the tide;

The middle phase, from line 5 to line 8, takes on a slightly different tone. Rather than an opening address as seen in the first four lines, we now hear a distinctly reflective tone and get the sense that the speaker's bitterness comes about because of painful memories:

> 5   The old snows melt from every mountain-side,
>   And last year's leaves are smoke in every lane;
>   But last year's bitter loving must remain
>   Heaped on my heart, and my old thoughts abide.

The closing phase of the poem shifts once more. The bitterness here is most interesting, because it is part of a conflicted emotion on the speaker's part – of painful ideas of loyalty to the lost loved one, which clash with the guilty relief of moving on:

There are a hundred places where I fear
10 To go,—so with his memory they brim.
And entering with relief some quiet place
Where never fell his foot or shone his face
I say, "There is no memory of him here!"
And so stand stricken, so remembering him.

So, in brief summary of the poem, what we have are various strong emotions arising from the poem itself. We see:

- **bitterness** in the **voice** and **tone** of the speaker
- **bitterness** at the **loss** (or death?) of the speaker's loved one
- the speaker's **anger** at those who have tried to advise her about the grieving process
- the speaker's **painful memories**
- the **conflicted emotions** of the speaker

Working through the poem quickly in this way means that we maintain our focus on the poem, but still keep the question in mind at all stages. It also gives us a variety of points, helping us to break down the topic of strong emotions fully.

Now, after this important preparation work, reading carefully, breaking the poem into manageable parts, focusing on the question at all times, and summarising with skill, we are in a good position to start a 5-part essay response to the question.

We must provide a brief, summary introduction (in the usual style), and then explore the poem in detail in the opening, middle, and closing phases, before concluding meaningfully.

Let's have a go!

Here's an attempt at an introduction. Here I have tried to include a number of the key words and ideas from our bullet-point list:

> **In the sonnet, 'Time does not bring relief', by Edna St Vincent Millay, we find a seemingly angry speaker, who is struggling to move on with her life after the loss of a loved one. A great bitterness pervades the poem in the harsh tones of the speaker and we see Millay carefully examine the lasting idea that with love and loss comes painful memories and conflicting emotions, particularly those of fear and guilt.**

Now that we have our introduction, we can examine the opening phase of the poem closely. Let's choose some of the key ideas from the first four lines in order to answer the question:

Answering an Essay Question

> Millay opens the poem with a powerful, short statement from the bitter speaker: 'Time does not bring relief' (line 1). This is not a hopeful, optimistic voice at all, as the stress falls heavily on the word 'not' in this sharp assertion. The typical idea about grieving is that time is a great healer – well, here Millay's speaker rejects this notion brutally, and the punctuation in the middle of the line means that the poem stops abruptly just after it starts, so the impact of this thought is stronger. This bitter tone is strengthened further in the second half of the line: 'you all have lied' (line 1), and it is clear that the speaker is most angry at those people (probably close friends or family) who have tried to comfort her by telling her that 'time would ease' (line 2) her pain. The tone of the speaker builds further in lines three and four as we hear two sharp confessions: 'I miss him...' (line 3), followed by 'I want him...' (line 4), with the desire for her lover's return a bitter impossibility. The water imagery in these lines also suggests the bitterness of the speaker's situation: 'the weeping of the rain' (line 3) is a personification, explaining the extent of the speaker's tears, and the 'shrinking of the tide' (line 4) once more gives a feeling of something diminishing, fading, and turning to nothingness.

We must seek to build on these ideas now as we turn to the middle phase. However, we want to try to develop some new points and ideas about the strong emotions in the poem:

> As the poem develops, the natural imagery continues. Here though, the images suggest ideas of slowly passing time and perishing: 'The old snows melt' (line 5) and 'last year's leaves are smoke' (line 6), emphasise this natural decay, something that the speaker then fittingly contrasts to her lost love. It seems as if there is some acceptance in the passing of these elements (like melting snow and dead leaves) which naturally fade and die. However, when the speaker thinks of her lost love, the tone is starkly different: 'But last year's bitter loving must remain' (line 7). The emotive word 'bitter' is stressed heavily here along with the ringing word 'must', indicating the permanence of the speaker's grief. Millay qualifies this with the statement that the speaker's 'old thoughts abide' (line 8), to give, once more, the impression of a bitter, lingering pain.

Answering an Essay Question

Now, we turn to the closing of the poem. Keeping 'bitterness' in mind, we want to build on the previous points but continue to say something new:

> **Millay brings the poem to a close by focusing on the speaker's fear and by moving on from more reflective thoughts in the middle phase. First, we learn of how people are associated with places. The speaker even exaggerates, stating that there are 'a hundred places' (line 9) which frighten her because they remind her of him. This idea extends into the final lines; however, Millay shows us a contrast – of how a new place, somewhere not associated with the lost love, can bring some 'relief' (line 11) from bitter thoughts. The powerful rhyme of 'quiet place' (line 11) with 'face' (line 12) reminds once more of the painful association of people and place in our memories. Here, however, we get the quiet sense of the man's absence in the soft alliteration: 'Where never fell his foot or shone his face' (line 12), which again links back to the speaker's relief. Quite clearly, at this stage in the poem, it is only through her discovery of new places where her love has never been, which will provide any sense of her moving on.**
>
> **All of this is undermined, however, by the closing two lines of the poem where a bitter irony pervades. Here, Millay shows a momentary sense of triumph on the speaker's part in the direct address: 'There is no memory of him here!' (line 13), as the speaker realises her only salvation from the grieving process might be to find new places to go (where the lover never set foot and where there might not be any painful associations attached). However, this is where the most bitter realisation occurs, as it is entirely because of his absence from these new places in her life, that the speaker is left in the closing image, 'stricken' (line 14) at the thought of his absence and therefore remains forever 'remembering him' (line 14) still. This is a devastating thought, giving the sense that the painful grief will never be over and that there is seemingly no escape from the loss of her lover.**

Let's try to review what we have discovered and provide a meaningful conclusion. Here, we can speculate on the writer's intentions and treatment of the theme, perhaps:

> **In conclusion, Millay describes very convincing, strong emotions and an overriding sense of bitterness throughout the poem,**

> particularly as she is keen to highlight the ongoing pain that is associated with love and loss. Overall, there appears to be little self-pity in Millay's speaker. She instead is an all-knowing figure who is angry at the world and everyone left in it – an enduringly bitter and grief-stricken person who is fully aware that she is impossibly trapped both by the painful memories of her past and the guilt of living on in a future without the person she loved.

A good way of understanding the structure of the essay itself is to go back now and read just the formal essay paragraphs straight through without the accompanying notes. This is made easier for you because the essay is written in a bold font, which means you can ignore the interrupting commentary in between. Doing this will enable you to feel and sense how the essay is constructed and how each paragraph flows into the next, from the introduction through to the conclusion.

Let's look at another poem now and have another go.

Here is a more modern, free-verse poem, 'Blessing', by the poet Imtiaz Dharker (1954–). Let's read carefully and then consider the piece in the light of the accompanying question:

How does the poet capture a <u>celebratory atmosphere</u> in the poem, 'Blessing'?

Blessing

by Imtiaz Dharker

>　　The skin cracks like a pod.
>　　There never is enough water.
>
>　　Imagine the drip of it,
>　　the small splash, echo
>5　in a tin mug,
>　　the voice of a kindly god.
>
>　　Sometimes, the sudden rush
>　　of fortune. The municipal pipe bursts,
>　　silver crashes to the ground
>10　and the flow has found
>　　a roar of tongues. From the huts,
>　　a congregation: every man woman
>　　child for streets around

butts in, with pots,
15　brass, copper, aluminium,
plastic buckets,
frantic hands,

and naked children
screaming in the liquid sun,
20　their highlights polished to perfection,
flashing light,
as the blessing sings
over their small bones.

One defining feature of this poem by Imtiaz Dharker is the use of free-verse form, and when reading, it becomes apparent that the irregularity of the line length, and the shorter lines in particular, do add to the speed and excitement of the poem. This is something that we might want to comment on, as it is important for us to consider how the poet's use of form impacts meaning when necessary. Here's an attempt at doing so in the introduction:

> **Imtiaz Dharker's free-verse poem, 'Blessing', is a celebration of water and the joy and relief it can bring to an impoverished community suffering from the desperate effects of drought. Dharker employs an effective third-person narrative perspective in order to create a sense of our observing the action, which takes place, live, before our eyes, as a water pipe bursts in the street and flocks of people come running excitedly to the site. This detached, voyeuristic point of view becomes an important aspect of the poem overall.**

Now we can explore the opening phase of the poem and, in order to answer the question, we should seek to evaluate the sense of celebration which is evident in the early lines:

The skin cracks like a pod.
There never is enough water.

Imagine the drip of it,
the small splash, echo
5　in a tin mug,
the voice of a kindly god.

What is interesting when we read the poem, is that Dharker structures her poem dramatically in order to give a joyless sense to the scene at the start. In terms of the question then, we would have to say that, quite honestly, no celebration is apparent at this early stage and so this fact has to form the basis of our commentary here.

> **Interestingly, as the poem opens, there is no sense of celebration at all. Instead, Dharker deliberately structures the poem with an abrupt start – a couplet, composed of two short, end-stopped lines. The first line is dry, clipped, and joyless in its monosyllabic statement: 'The skin cracks like a pod' (line 1). The metaphor here describes the earth as a 'skin', parched and wrinkled, and the dynamic verb 'crack' suggests a severe fracturing of the landscape, exaggerated further by its harsh onomatopoeic sound. This opening line, is qualified by the next despairing assertion: 'There never is enough water' (line 2). However, in the second stanza, the tone of the poem starts to lift. The word 'imagine' (line 3) provides the beginning of more hopeful things to come. Dharker's speaker, through a gentle imperative, invites us to 'Imagine the drip of it' (line 3), a drop of water, which will make a 'small splash' (line 4) when caught in the 'tin mug' (line 5). All the sound effects here are gentle and precise, 'drip of it' is a teasing assonance, mimicking the tiny echo of a falling drop of water, which turns into the softly sibilant 'small splash' which hits the hard consonant of the 'tin'. The words in lines 4 to 5 here are all monosyllables again – and through this, Dharker manages to create a very slow, deliberate action of a single drop of water falling. The imagery is very precise and focused around the sound here, as the poet likens this hopeful sign of water to 'the voice of a kindly god' (line 6). This is the starting point for the extended metaphor of the 'blessing' (of the ceremonial holy water) which carries through the rest of the poem.**

From this point on, we find that Dharker's poem truly becomes celebratory in the middle to closing phases of the poem:

>   Sometimes, the sudden rush
>   of fortune. The municipal pipe bursts,
>   silver crashes to the ground
> 10 and the flow has found
>   a roar of tongues. From the huts,
>   a congregation: every man woman
>   child for streets around

butts in, with pots,
15 brass, copper, aluminium,
plastic buckets,
frantic hands,

It is important for us to consider the structural impact of this in the following section of our answer, therefore. Once more, when evaluating the middle phase of the poem, we want to try to consider how ideas and themes are developing from the opening phase, and of how language and images are building up, becoming layered, patterned, or contrasted:

> In the middle phase of the poem, the long stanza 3, Dharker increases the intensity of the action and the pace of the scene, most notably through enjambment, a series of run-on lines, and extensive listing. The phrase 'sudden rush' with its fast 'uh' sounding assonance and swift sibilance, starts the dramatic sequence of events. On line 8 the village comes alive as 'the municipal pipe bursts' and its water pours forth. Dharker compares the drops to 'silver' (line 9), suggesting both the light reflections and the figurative value of the water as it 'crashes to the ground' (line 9). The verb 'crashes' is dynamic and is quickly followed by the fluid fricative alliteration: 'and the flow has found / a roar of tongues' (lines 10 to 11). The enjambment also gives real speed and momentum in this passage of the poem and the timely caesura in line 11, creates a moment's necessary breather. The 'roar of tongues' – an image which describes the wild excitement and instinctive celebration of the village folk who come rushing as a 'congregation' (line 12) from the 'huts' (line 11) is truly evocative. 'Congregation' gives the sense of a church gathering, a community in excited ceremonial celebration – this religious image also brings us back to the important title, 'Blessing', as the extended metaphor begins to take shape.
>
> From this line 13 onward, after the caesura, Dharker employs short lines, listing, and fast-paced enjambment once more to give a sense of the 'frantic' (line 17) scene which takes place as the villagers, suffering the long-term effects of drought come rushing for the fountain of water. It is an excited moment, with all manner of people ('every man woman / child for streets around' of lines 11 and 12) fighting for the chance to catch the precious droplets in whichever vessel (the 'pots / brass, copper, aluminium, / plastic buckets' of lines 14 to 16) is nearest to hand. To continue the frenetic speed of the scene, Dharker runs on the third stanza into the fourth without stopping.

Answering an Essay Question 97

As noted before, we must pay close attention to the closing lines and images of the poem:

> and naked children
> screaming in the liquid sun,
> 20   their highlights polished to perfection,
> flashing light,
> as the blessing sings
> over their small bones.

We must bring our notes and observations constantly back to the question, however:

> **The closing moments of the poem are truly celebratory as Dharker creates a series of intense light images to give a sense of climactic joy to the scene. Dharker focuses on a picture of innocence: the 'naked children' (line 18) who are 'screaming' (line 19) with absolute abandon at their fortune 'in the liquid sun' (line 19) – a fitting metaphor which extends the water and light imagery here into the next line: of the 'highlights' (line 20) which reflect from the children, exaggeratedly 'polished to perfection' (line 20). The lines continue to run on and shorten dramatically. The 'flashing light' (line 21) is termed a 'blessing' (linking back to the title) which 'sings' (line 22) kindly, softly even, over the 'small bones' (line 23) of the village children. Their diminutive size once more highlights the innocence and fragility of the children in the moment.**

Now, we can attempt a meaningful conclusion by evaluating the craft and techniques of the poet. We are trying to answer the question of how effective Dharker has been in creating a celebratory feeling in 'Blessing'.

> **In conclusion, we see how through her skilful use of enjambment from line 7 of the poem to the very end, Dharker creates a real sense of speed and action in her poem, primarily through her control of the generally short-lined, free-verse form. The celebration is seen throughout as we move from a vivid picture of hardship and drought at the start of the poem to the exploding water pipe and the excited onrush of people into the scene. The celebration in the climax of the poem coexists with the feelings of joy and relief, and the 'blessing'**

> both metaphorically and literally experienced is achieved through a range of positive water and light imagery, artfully layered, line upon line. Because of the unique narrative perspective (the onlooking third-person view) throughout, we are not part of the celebration, but witnessing it. It is a private celebration, therefore – a blessing for those who desperately deserve it.

Once again, in the fashion of the previous essay examples, if you are keen to read the essay in full, go back now and read over the passages in bold font, ignoring the interrupting commentary in between the essay itself. This is a good practice, in order to sense the overall flow of the essay as it builds from the introduction to the conclusion. This will also help you prepare for the practice section to follow.

Practice

In this practice section, we have two new poems, each with an accompanying question.

Be sure to read the poem closely, before carefully considering which are the opening, middle, and closing phases of the poem.

Remember to build your answer around the 5-part model, and always keep the question in mind.

How does Elizabeth Barrett Browning (1806–1861) present ideas about love in the poem, 'How do I love thee?'?

Sonnets from the Portuguese 43: How do I love thee? Let me count the ways

by Elizabeth Barrett Browning

> How do I love thee? Let me count the ways.
> I love thee to the depth and breadth and height
> My soul can reach, when feeling out of sight
> For the ends of being and ideal grace.
> 5 I love thee to the level of every day's
> Most quiet need, by sun and candle-light.
> I love thee freely, as men strive for right;
> I love thee purely, as they turn from praise.
> I love thee with the passion put to use
> 10 In my old griefs, and with my childhood's faith.
> I love thee with a love I seemed to lose

With my lost saints. I love thee with the breath,
Smiles, tears, of all my life; and, if God choose,
I shall but love thee better after death.

How does Frances Ellen Watkins Harper (1825–1911) present a sense of <u>triumph</u> in the poem 'Learning to Read'?

Learning to Read

by Frances Ellen Watkins Harper

    Very soon the Yankee teachers
        Came down and set up school;
    But, oh! how the Rebs did hate it,—
        It was agin' their rule.

5   Our masters always tried to hide
        Book learning from our eyes;
    Knowledge didn't agree with slavery—
        'Twould make us all too wise.

    But some of us would try to steal
10   A little from the book,
    And put the words together,
        And learn by hook or crook.

    I remember Uncle Caldwell,
        Who took pot-liquor fat
15 And greased the pages of his book,
        And hid it in his hat.

    And had his master ever seen
        The leaves up on his head,
    He'd have thought them greasy papers,
20   But nothing to be read.

    And there was Mr. Turner's Ben,
        Who heard the children spell,
    And picked the words right up by heart,
        And learned to read 'em well.

25 Well, the Northern folks kept sending
        The Yankee teachers down;

And they stood right up and helped us,
    Though Rebs did sneer and frown.

And, I longed to read my Bible,
30   For precious words it said;
But when I begun to learn it,
    Folks just shook their heads,

And said there is no use trying,
    Oh! Chloe, you're too late;
35 But as I was rising sixty,
    I had no time to wait.

So I got a pair of glasses,
    And straight to work I went,
And never stopped till I could read
40   The hymns and Testament.

Then I got a little cabin—
    A place to call my own—
And I felt as independent
    As the queen upon her throne.

7 Comparing Poems

Another challenge we are faced with in our study of poetry is when we try to compare two poems together.

In conversation or discussion this is not such an overwhelming task. People are often happy to state that they like one poem or poet more than another. They might simply have an instinctive preference for one over the other or they might even begin to explain why one poem could be deemed better than another too.

And when comparing poems in essays, we essentially use the same principles: that of keeping two texts in mind simultaneously, of commenting on one poem and then another, using all manner of comparative statements along the way.

The greatest difference, however, is that in more formal essays, when we compare poems on the written page, we are likely to move away from overtly subjective, personal comments to a more technical and technique-based commentary.

This chapter ultimately shows how we can do this. Once more, we will explore the 5-part essay method, and demonstrate how we can use it effectively to compare two poems.

Let's begin!

Consider the following essay question and the two accompanying poems:

Compare how Elizabeth Jennings (1926–2001) and Katherine Philips (1632–1664) present <u>attitudes to death</u> in the poems 'For a Child Born Dead' and 'On the Death of My First and Dearest Child'.

For a Child Born Dead

by Elizabeth Jennings

> What ceremony can we fit
> You into now? If you had come
> Out of a warm and noisy room
> To this, there'd be an opposite
> 5 For us to know you by. We could
> Imagine you in lively mood.

DOI: 10.4324/9781003207511-8

And then look at the other side,
The mood drawn out of you, the breath
Defeated by the power of death.
10 But we have never seen you stride
Ambitiously the world we know.
You could not come and yet you go.

But there is nothing now to mar
Your clear refusal of our world.
15 Not in our memories can we mould
You or distort your character.
Then all our consolation is
That grief can be as pure as this.

On the Death of My First and Dearest Child, Hector Philips, born the 23rd of April, and died the 2nd of May 1655.

by Katherine Philips

Twice forty months in wedlock I did stay,
   Then had my vows crowned with a lovely boy.
And yet in forty days he dropped away;
   O swift vicissitude of human joy!

5 I did but see him, and he disappeared,
   I did but touch the rosebud, and it fell;
A sorrow unforeseen and scarcely feared,
   So ill can mortals their afflictions spell.

And now (sweet babe) what can my trembling heart
10   Suggest to right my doleful fate or thee?
Tears are my muse, and sorrow all my art,
   So piercing groans must be thy elegy.

Thus whilst no eye is witness of my moan,
   I grieve thy loss (ah, boy too dear to live!)
15 And let the unconcerned world alone,
   Who neither will, nor can refreshment give.

An offering too for thy sad tomb I have,
   Too just a tribute to thy early hearse;
Receive these gasping numbers to thy grave,
20   The last of thy unhappy mother's verse.

Now, where do we start? This can be quite a daunting moment. We have just read two new poems and we have a lot of information to process before we can begin.

The great danger here, with so much information to hand, is to panic and simply dive straight in, making all manner of observations about what we have just read. However, what quickly happens with this approach is that we lose any structure of our thoughts and often we lose a sense of balance between the poems, typically commenting on one poem more than the other.

Well, the key aspects of an effective poetry comparison are *structure* and *balance* – by structure we mean the way that we build and present our points, and by balance we mean how fairly or equally weighted our comments about each poem are.

There are many ways to structure a poetry comparison. In order to create true balance in an answer, some people like to comment on one poem first, before turning their attention to the second poem and pointing out the relevant comparisons and contrasts as the essay proceeds.

Perhaps a more sophisticated way of writing poetry comparisons is by using an interweaving method, where we make continuous comparisons and contrasts between the two poems throughout the essay itself.

The 5-part essay method really helps here, and we will explore how to use this method closely now. To start, let's take a bit of time to focus on each poem separately, in its own right. Let's try to manage our general thoughts about each poem, and then consider how these might apply to the theme of 'attitudes to death'.

Let's have a look at the first poem, 'For a Child Born Dead', by Elizabeth Jennings. In this modern poem we have a first person speaker, who shares some sort of relationship with the stillborn child of the title. She speaks throughout in the plural 'we', so we can assume that the speaker is one of the collective mourners perhaps, of a parent, but more likely of a relative or a friend – it is a shared pain, after all, that Jennings describes. The speaker also addresses the dead child directly with a question at the start, and the poem has a sad sense of the speaker's imagining of what the child's life could have been like if it had managed to survive.

With these general notes in mind, here is a brief summary of the poem:

> **'For a Child Born Dead' by Elizabeth Jennings is written from the perspective of someone mourning (a close family member or a friend, perhaps) who addresses the dead child in an attempt to deal with her grief. The speaker in the poem is strong in the face of this tragedy, however, and manages somehow to accept what has happened.**

104   *Comparing Poems*

This is fine for now, but let's turn to the poem 'On the Death of My First and Dearest Child' by Katherine Philips and try a similar approach. First, we can read the poem and make some brief observations. This time, however, we should also try to keep Jennings's poem 'For A Child Born Dead' in mind, because we can start to make some comparisons and contrasts even at this early stage.

In Philips's poem, one that is written over 300 years before Jennings's, it is strikingly clear this time we have a grieving mother speaking the lines. Philips' poem is very personal as the boy, Hector, is named in the title and we know this to be the poet's son. If we turn back to the first poem, 'For a Child Born Dead', we do not know for a fact that Jennings is writing from her own experience of losing a child – we can only assume that because of the emotionally distanced speaker that this is not from a mother's point of view. This, along with the stark time difference, forms the obvious contrast between the poems and suggests why the tones are so different.

These are important things to consider later, but for now, let's return to 'On the Death of My First and Dearest Child' and attempt a brief summary:

> **In Katherine Philips' elegy 'On the Death of My First and Dearest Child', we hear the poet lamenting the loss of her baby boy. We learn of the shock of his death to her and the unhappiness she is left with in the wake of her son's passing.**

So now, we have two general summaries of the separate poems and a clear understanding of each, we can try to combine them into a brief introduction for our essay.

A good way of doing this is to use statements which show both similarities and difference at the same time. The 'both-but' statement is an effective tool for this and helps us form clear comparative comments. Here we can start by thinking about both poems immediately, before branching off and looking at how they are uniquely different.

This is an attempt at an introduction, using a 'both-but' statement:

> **Both Elizabeth Jennings and Katherine Philips, in their respective poems 'For a Child Born Dead' and 'On the Death of My First and Dearest Child', present sorrowful speakers who are coming to terms with the painful fact of a child's death. With Jennings, we find how a modern poet treats this hardship through an emotionally distanced speaker, but with Philips (a poet of the 17th Century) we discover how she creates a picture of raw, maternal grief in a personal elegy for her own son. With a time span of over 300 years between the poems, we**

> **can begin to consider the very different positions of the speakers and learn how poetry through the ages has continued to treat such a timeless issue as child death in all manner of sensitive ways.**

It is a fairly short introduction and is written to just over 100 words. This is important, because we do not want to write too much in the introduction or provide too much detail – we are simply trying to set up the essay and give a general sense of the poems and the question at hand, only touching on how the poems are similar and different on the surface.

As the essay proceeds, we can add a lot more specific detail.

Let's look at the openings of each poem now. In this case, 'For a Child Born Dead' is a poem which naturally divides into three stanzas, so here we can concentrate our attention on the opening stanza. With the poem, 'On the Death of My First and Dearest Child', the poem is in five stanzas, so we need to make a judgement about where the opening, middle, and closing phases of the poem are, in order for us to adopt the 5-part essay structure. After a review of 'On the Death of My First and Dearest Child', it is evident that the first two stanzas form the opening because the third stanza signals the change of the speaker's address to the child, and the final two stanzas are then the closing thoughts of the speaker of the poem.

So to begin, we can look again at stanza 1 of 'For a Child Born Dead':

> What ceremony can we fit
> You into now? If you had come
> Out of a warm and noisy room
> To this, there'd be an opposite
> 5   For us to know you by. We could
> Imagine you in lively mood.

Next we can reread stanzas 1 and 2 of 'On the Death of My First and Dearest Child':

> Twice forty months in wedlock I did stay,
>   Then had my vows crowned with a lovely boy.
> And yet in forty days he dropped away;
>   O swift vicissitude of human joy!
>
> 5   I did but see him, and he disappeared,
>   I did but touch the rosebud, and it fell;
>   A sorrow unforeseen and scarcely feared,
>   So ill can mortals their afflictions spell.

106   *Comparing Poems*

Now we can attempt some detailed comparisons. Here are some general observations from which we can build our answer:

'For a Child Born Dead' starts with a direct address from the speaker to the deceased child. Jennings opens with the **rhetorical question**, which remains unanswered. The poet also uses the conditional tense ('If you had come') to imagine the future of the child that has been lost. The key emotive word in this opening is 'Imagine' on line 6. Interestingly the speaker talks of 'we', so we have a sense that the speaker is also speaking on behalf of other people and mourners too.

Turning to 'On the Death of My First and Dearest Child, Hector Philips, born the 23rd of April, and died the 2nd of May 1655' – the full title needs some consideration, as does the fact that the poem starts with the speaker (the mother) contemplating her personal loss, particularly focusing on time – the length of marriage and the expectancy of the son compared to the shortness of his life. Also, we have painful descriptions of the fragility of the baby's life, and the emotive word which defines the opening of the poem is 'sorrow' on line 7.

So, we have some things to work with. Now, we can attempt to bring these notes together in a bit more detail. First, we will explore 'For a Child Born Dead' and then we will turn to 'On the Death of My First and Dearest Child'. Try to note the words and phrases (the **discourse markers**) which signal these moments of comparison:

> In 'For a Child Born Dead', for example, Jennings opens the poem with a despondent rhetorical question. The speaker asks the stillborn baby directly: 'What ceremony can we fit / You into now?' (lines 1 to 2), with the obvious answer being none. We are left immediately then with an impression of wearied hopelessness and despair, reminded that with the end of life comes no future 'ceremony', save only the child's funeral. The use of the plural pronoun 'we' is important here, as we get a sense of the collective suffering at the child's death, as if Jennings, through her speaker, is able to consider and speak for all manner of mourners involved (of family, friends, and even more distant connections to the child). This is followed by a poignant use of the conditional tone. Jennings shows how the speaker contemplates a different reality, in which the child had survived: 'If you had come / Out of a warm and noisy room / To this' (line 4). We might think of the cosy 'room' here to be a metaphor for the mother's womb, as the baby is born into life – 'opposite' (line 4) to the cold and cruel events of its death. The whimsical tone of the speaker in the opening of 'For a Child Born Dead' is moving and at the end of the first stanza we are drawn to the emotive word

'Imagine' (line 6) and the carefully chosen adjective 'lively' (line 6) as we picture her, still dreaming of a future for the child that will never be.

In contrast to this, the speaker in 'On the Death of My First and Dearest Child' is the overt voice of a grieving mother, and we are drawn immediately to the precise dates which Philips uses in the full title in order to commemorate her dead son, Hector. It reads, fittingly for an elegy, in the formal diction of a headstone: 'Hector Philips, born the 23rd of April, and died the 2nd of May 1655'. Now, the fact of the poet's writing in the middle of the 1600s meant that infant mortality was quite common, and was even a natural part of life in the poet's time. However, what Philips seeks to demonstrate in her poem is the very human, personal grief any mother would feel at such a loss – she seems to accept that there is little care from the outside world for her sorrow and so chooses instead to focus on her own pity at the death of her boy. She writes of how after a mere 'forty days he dropped away' (line 3). In this brutal image, 'dropped', we feel the suddenness of the loss and the mother's inability to hold on to her son. As a result, in the following exclamation, the mother states how painfully 'swift' the 'human joy'(line 4) of motherhood was for her. It is this fact, which forms the stark contrast between the speakers' attitudes to death and the overall tones of the poems. Whereas the sorrowful tone of the speaker in 'For a Child Born Dead' arrives as a gentle musing about the life the dead child might have had (an attitude which suggests that the speaker is a close friend or relation, rather than the mother herself), Philips, in 'On the Death of My First and Dearest Child' instead develops further the mother's desperate, angrier tones, through repeated images of powerlessness. In the second stanza, the effective caesura in both lines 5 and 6 creates a balance between the mother's vain attempt to 'see' and 'touch' her son against the impact of his sudden death. Philips writes: 'I did but see him, and he disappeared, / I did but touch the rosebud, and it fell'. The boy being likened to an unopened flower that fails to bloom is a fitting metaphor which suggests the fragility and shortness of his life here.

So, as we can see, at this stage in the essay, we have managed to evaluate the openings of both poems and we have taken the time to comment on each poem in rich detail, while still making comparisons and contrasts between them too. It is a bit of a juggling act, but with practice, it becomes easier.

108 *Comparing Poems*

We can now move on to the middle phase of both poems. For clarity, let's continue to deal with Jennings's poem 'For a Child Born Dead' first, and follow with 'On the Death of My First and Dearest Child'. We do this, so that we can narrow our focus of each poem and provide good, detailed observations without rushing.

As noted before, we can look at stanza 2 of 'For a Child Born Dead':

> And then look at the other side,
> The mood drawn out of you, the breath
> Defeated by the power of death.
> 10 But we have never seen you stride
> Ambitiously the world we know.
> You could not come and yet you go.

Next, we can reread stanza 3 of 'On the Death of My First and Dearest Child':

> And now (sweet babe) what can my trembling heart
> 10   Suggest to right my doleful fate or thee?
> Tears are my muse, and sorrow all my art,
>   So piercing groans must be thy elegy.

Now, the interesting thing about the middle phase of 'For a Child Born Dead' is that we turn from the imagined life to the reality. Stanza 2 of Jennings's poem is hard-hitting and in contrast to the more gentle tones of the first stanza. The stanza ends on a hard statement of acceptance.

And, when we look at 'On the Death of My first and Dearest Child' we find a similar tonal shift has happened; however, in this poem, the shift comes in the form of the mother's bitter words in the opening, turning to the mother's direct address to the dead child in the form of a rhetorical question (a technique we have already seen the other poet, Jennings, use).

Right, let's work on these notes and make some points:

> **As both poems develop into the middle phase, it is clear that the different tones of the speakers shift accordingly, but where the speaker in 'For a Child Born Dead' continues to accept the reality of the death of the stillborn baby, the mother in 'On the Death of My First and Dearest Child' becomes increasingly disturbed, and the poem intensifies in its descriptions of grief and pain. For example, in the second stanza of 'For a Child Born Dead', the speaker turns away from her dreaming and begins to look at 'the other side' (line 5) – the reality of the baby's death. We have some insight into the grieving process here, and it is interesting to note how such euphemistic**

language is used when discussing harsh matters of death – this, after all, is the sort of language that those in mourning use to console each other. The images which follow are subtle, yet stark, showing how life is slowly taken away. Jennings writes that the 'mood' is 'drawn out' of the child on line 8, and rhymes 'breath' (line 9) with 'death' (line 10) to give a sense of the closeness between the last, slow act of breathing and that of passing away. Added to this, on line 9, we feel the speaker's sense of the force of death in the heavy alliteration on the plosive 'd' and 'p' sounds in the full line: 'Defeated by the power of death'. Even though the reality is a difficult one for the speaker, the final images, in keeping with the overall mood of this poem, are still gentle, yet poignant. To linger on phrases like 'we have never seen you stride / Ambitiously' (lines 10 to 11) acknowledges how any sense of future pride has been taken away from the parents, the family and friends too, ending with the bold statement in a single, end-stopped line: 'You could not come and yet you go' (line 12). All words here are slow, heavy-hitting monosyllables, ending on the sad, resigned thought – 'yet you go'.

However, as we turn to Philips's 'On the Death of My First and Dearest Child', we find that the speaker's very personal despair and anger build dramatically in stanza 3. Just as we saw in Jennings's poem, Philips also uses direct address effectively in the form of a rhetorical question; however, rather than starting the poem with an intimate question to the child in the style of 'For a Child Born Dead', Philips instead intensifies the voice of the grieving mother by using it in the middle of her poem to show how distraught and lost the mother really becomes. The timing of the question gives a sense of her helplessness, futilely asking: 'And now (sweet babe) what can my trembling heart / Suggest to right my doleful fate or thee?' (lines 9 to 10). It is a hopeless plea, with the obvious answer one of total negativity: nothing. We should focus on the possessive pronoun 'my' here, as an indication of the mother's personal suffering and read of the speaker's self-confessed 'trembling heart' (line 9), of her 'tears' and 'sorrow' (line 11) and 'piercing groans' (line 12), and how these sufferings become the 'muse' (line 11) or inspiration for the poem for her dead son – for his 'elegy' (line 12).

We have now made some comprehensive comparisons and noted some obvious contrasts. Let's finish effectively by evaluating the closing phases of each poem in a similar style.

110 *Comparing Poems*

Here is the final stanza of 'For a Child Born Dead':

> But there is nothing now to mar
> Your clear refusal of our world.
> 15 Not in our memories can we mould
> You or distort your character.
> Then all our consolation is
> That grief can be as pure as this.

Next, are the final two stanzas of 'On the Death of My First and Dearest Child':

> Thus whilst no eye is witness of my moan,
>   I grieve thy loss (ah, boy too dear to live!)
> 15 And let the unconcerned world alone,
>   Who neither will, nor can refreshment give.
>
> An offering too for thy sad tomb I have,
>   Too just a tribute to thy early hearse;
> Receive these gasping numbers to thy grave,
> 20   The last of thy unhappy mother's verse.

Here are the general notes:

In 'For a Child Born Dead' Jennings's speaker continues to address the dead child, and the overall tone of the poem remains calm and accepting. The final stanza of the poem is made up of three statements essentially (note the three full stops) which end on a note of 'consolation'.

When turning to 'On the Death of My First and Dearest Child', the tone of the poem also calms in a marked way, with the speaker feeling isolated and seemingly left alone to her grief – her final gesture is her offering of the poem itself to her son.

We can attempt to write up these thoughts in greater detail now:

> **As Jennings's brings 'For a Child Born Dead' to a close, we find that there is a general slowing down and a feeling of final acceptance in the speaker at the loss of the child. The language throughout the final stanza is gentle too and the speaker somehow manages to view the untimely death in a positive light, ultimately concluding that the 'refusal' (line 14) of life was entirely the child's own choosing, and that because of the tragic early death, the stillborn babe**

has been spared the corrupting influences of human existence – the speaker gropes for any positive, comforting thought, stating: 'Not in our memories can we mould / You or distort your character' (lines 15 to 16). The irony here is that all memory, both positive and negative, has been denied the collective mourners in this instance, having 'never seen' (line 10) or known the child. The final statement in the poem is another half-convincing one – however, it is a show of strength and an attempt at truly accepting the hard truth, that the only 'consolation' (line 17) is that their 'grief' (line 18), in light of never having met the child, is extreme in a sense, and therefore entirely 'pure' (line 18).

In similar style, 'On the Death of My First and Dearest Child', seems to slow down in pace at the close as if the mother has all but exhausted herself with her emotional outpouring. What we find in contrast to Jennings, however, is that the grieving is one of solitary mourning, as the mother lets 'the unconcerned world alone' (line 15). Another painful truth we find in Philips's account is in the details of her marriage and the lack of support from her husband. The 'twice forty months in wedlock' (line 1) that the speaker seems to have endured to achieve the 'lovely boy' (line 2) is bitterly qualified in stanza 4 by the reality of the loneliness she now suffers in her grief. The supportive husband figure is absent as 'no eye is witness' (line 13) to her private suffering. This is a moment's self-pity, but perhaps a fair criticism of marriage and attitudes to child death at the time of Philips's writing, describing an unfeeling world, which cares little for a mother's suffering in the wake of such a traumatising, yet common, experience; a thought which seems to contrast with the sentiment in Jennings's more modern poem, where her compassionate speaker, through the continued use of the plural pronouns ('we', 'us', 'our') attempts to show how grief of this kind can be shared. Instead, as a further way of coping with the tragic death, Philips's speaker in 'On the Death of My First and Dearest Child' offers up the poem itself ('these gasping numbers' on line 19) to the memory of her son as 'a tribute' (line 18), vowing never to write again, perhaps because there is no fitting subject left to her after all this. As a lasting reminder, the speaker describes herself in the final line as an 'unhappy mother' (line 18) – once more, giving a raw and open confession of her true self, in the wake of her boy's death.

112 Comparing Poems

After all of this work, we are now ready to conclude meaningfully. Let's try to make overall points of similarity and contrast by keeping both poems in mind and by reviewing the subtle differences between them. The conclusion is also a good opportunity to consider further the writers' methods and possible intentions. We should continue to work with the 'both-but' statements here, as a way of keeping the poems' similarities and differences clearly defined.

> **To conclude, it is evident that both 'For a Child Born Dead' and 'On the Death of My First and Dearest Child' are painful accounts of grief at the loss of a child, that the periods in which they were written and the contexts for each are significant. Throughout 'For a Child Born Dead' Jennings maintains a degree of reflective acceptance in the voice of the speaker, perhaps because the loss described is a collective one, evoking a quiet strength in the figure, as a compassionate mourner – this perhaps is the lasting impression of Jennings's work, particularly in the stoical tones of the final stanza. Contrastingly, the despair seen in Philips's speaker is demonstrative and raw, rather than quiet and understated, purely because we hear the explicit lament of a devastated mother throughout. It is probably fair to say that the gestures of love and grief as seen in 'For a Child Born Dead' are just as sincere as the ones seen in 'On the Death of My First and Dearest Child'; however, they are completely different because of the immediate and visceral pain we witness in Philips's personal account. What we find with the two poems is ultimately a portrait of shattered hope in the struggle for acceptance in the face of terrible tragedy – with both speakers finding a way of coping with the harsh realities of child death on their own terms.**

Once more, in order to appreciate the structure of the essay in full, it is worthwhile taking the time to go back now and to read through the essay paragraphs without the interrupting notes. Follow the paragraphs in the bold font, reading from the introduction through to the conclusion, and try to sense how the 5-part method works in action.

Next, to consolidate our understanding of this comparison method, let's look at two more poems to a given theme.

In this comparison essay, we see the presentation of two fathers by Paul Laurence Dunbar (1872–1906) and Ben Jonson (1572–1637). The essay question we will work to is:

How do the poets present <u>father figures</u> in 'Little Brown Baby' and 'On My First Son'?

Little Brown Baby

by Paul Laurence Dunbar

    Little brown baby wif spa'klin' eyes,
    Come to yo' pappy an' set on his knee.
    What you been doin', suh — makin' san' pies?
    Look at dat bib — you's es du'ty ez me.
5 Look at dat mouf — dat's merlasses, I bet;
    Come hyeah, Maria, an' wipe off his han's.
    Bees gwine to ketch you an' eat you up yit,
    Bein' so sticky an sweet — goodness lan's!

    Little brown baby wif spa'klin' eyes,
10 Who's pappy's darlin' an' who's pappy's chile?
    Who is it all de day nevah once tries
    Fu' to be cross, er once loses dat smile?
    Whah did you git dem teef? My, you's a scamp!
    Whah did dat dimple come f'om in yo' chin?
15 Pappy do' know you — I b'lieves you's a tramp;
    Mammy, dis hyeah's some ol' straggler got in!

    Let's th'ow him outen de do' in de san',
    We do' want stragglers a-layin' 'roun' hyeah;
    Let's gin him 'way to de big buggah-man;
20 I know he's hidin' erroun' hyeah right neah.
    Buggah-man, buggah-man, come in de do',
    Hyeah's a bad boy you kin have fu' to eat.
    Mammy an' pappy do' want him no mo',
    Swaller him down f'om his haid to his feet!

25 Dah, now, I t'ought dat you'd hug me up close.
    Go back, ol' buggah, you sha'n't have dis boy.
    He ain't no tramp, ner no straggler, of co'se;
    He's pappy's pa'dner an' play-mate an' joy.
    Come to you' pallet now — go to yo' res';
30 Wisht you could allus know ease an' cleah skies;
    Wisht you could stay jes' a chile on my breas'—
    Little brown baby wif spa'klin' eyes!

On My First Son

by Ben Jonson

Farewell, thou child of my right hand, and joy;
My sin was too much hope of thee, lov'd boy.
Seven years tho' wert lent to me, and I thee pay,
Exacted by thy fate, on the just day.
5   O, could I lose all father now! For why
Will man lament the state he should envy?
To have so soon 'scap'd world's and flesh's rage,
And if no other misery, yet age?
Rest in soft peace, and, ask'd, say, "Here doth lie
10   Ben Jonson his best piece of poetry."
For whose sake henceforth all his vows be such,
As what he loves may never like too much.

First, as in the style of the other poetry comparison, let's make some general observations about each poem, and then attempt to bring the notes together for an introduction.

Here are some of my notes:

When reading Dunbar's poem to his son the first obvious feature is that the speaker is the father addressing his baby directly. It is written in an informal, playful **dialect**. The colloquial language is lively and dramatic and suggests the ease and comfort of the father in the company of his boy. The situation of the poem seems to take place at the dinner table, at feeding time, as 'Mammy' and 'Pappy' are present in the scene and the child has become quite messy. We can note that Dunbar uses a series of questions throughout his poem from father to son; this is done in an amusing way as the baby obviously cannot respond. There is a growing sense of the father's playful teasing of the boy and the explicit use of the word 'joy' in praise of his son. The poem ends on the parents putting the boy to bed, ending in the hope of a peaceful rest.

To summarise Dunbar's poem then:

> **'Little Brown Baby' by Paul Laurence Dunbar is a playful poem, in which a loving father speaks directly to his baby son. In a very lively and dramatic scene, which takes place at the baby's feeding time, Dunbar describes the father's excited tones and sense of joy in the company of his little boy.**

Let's turn to Ben Jonson's poem now and write down some general observations. We must remember, however, to keep Dunbar's poem in mind too. Here are some notes:

First, when reading 'On My First Son' we also find that this poem describes a father speaking directly to his son. The contrast already is that in Jonson's **elegy**, he is addressing his dead son, who has died at the age of seven years old. The tone of the piece is serious and mournful. However, in direct comparison to Dunbar, we find the poet describing his son as his 'joy'. Also we get the sense that Jonson's poem is a valediction – a farewell. In an interesting image, Jonson likens his son to a piece of poetry as a fitting compliment. We see the poet also using rhetorical questions, but Johnson's poem, in complete contrast to Dunbar's, uses them to show the speaker's fundamental despair.

With these notes in mind, we can attempt a summary of the poem:

> **'On My First Son' is Ben Jonson's elegy for his seven-year-old son. It is written from the father to the son and has a serious, mournful tone throughout. In many ways it is Jonson's valediction and opportunity both to praise and say goodbye to the child he loved.**

Now we are in a position to take our separate summaries and bring them together into a brief introduction for the essay.

Here's an attempt at an introduction, using a 'both-but' statement:

> **Both Paul Laurence Dunbar and Ben Jonson, in their respective poems, 'Little Brown Baby' and 'On My First Son', describe affectionate and loving father figures. But, where Dunbar, in his lively and dramatic piece, shows how joyful fatherhood can be in a playful, domestic scene at feeding time with his little boy, Jonson instead shows the great tragedy of fatherhood, as he describes his feelings of pride and personal pain in his moving elegy for the death of his eldest child, his seven-year-old son.**

Again, the skill here is to write succinctly, to around 100 words. Also, the order in which we address the poems here is important, as we will seek to maintain this first-poem/second-poem dynamic (of Dunbar and then Jonson) throughout the essay for clarity and structure.

Now, we must consider the opening, middle, and closing phases of each poem, in order to construct the body of our 5-part essay.

We can note that Dunbar's poem is made of four octaves (eight-line stanzas) and Jonson's elegy is composed of 12 lines. Each of Dunbar's stanzas are contained with full stops at the end; therefore we can treat stanza 1 as the opening of the poem, stanzas 2 and 3, as the middle, and stanza 4 as the closing phase.

116   *Comparing Poems*

With Jonson's poem, when looking at the natural stopping points, we find that the poem is essentially constructed in three quatrains, so lines 1 to 4 form the opening, lines 5 to 8 form the middle, and lines 9 to 12 form the closing. We will use our understanding of the respective phases in order to make our comparisons between the two poems now.

So, let's look more closely at the presentations of the father figures in stanza 1 of 'Little Brown Baby' and the first four lines of 'On My First Son'.

Here is the opening of Dunbar's poem:

> Little brown baby wif spa'klin' eyes,
> Come to yo' pappy an' set on his knee.
> What you been doin', suh — makin' san' pies?
> Look at dat bib — you's es du'ty ez me.
> 5   Look at dat mouf — dat's merlasses, I bet;
> Come hyeah, Maria, an' wipe off his han's.
> Bees gwine to ketch you an' eat you up yit,
> Bein' so sticky an sweet — goodness lan's!

And here is the opening of Jonson's elegy:

> Farewell, thou child of my right hand, and joy;
> My sin was too much hope of thee, lov'd boy.
> Seven years tho' wert lent to me, and I thee pay,
> Exacted by thy fate, on the just day.

Now, after reading both passages, we might make observations along the following lines:

> **In the opening stanza of Dunbar's 'Little Brown Baby' the first defining feature of the father figure is the way he talks to his son directly. Dunbar uses dialect words to add a natural warmth and ease of voice to the father. Gentle instructions are seen in the imperatives: 'Come to yo' pappy an' set on his knee' (line 2), and the situation of the poem is established immediately as the little baby is placed lovingly in the father's lap. The first question then arrives on line 3 as the father addresses his son in mock formal tones: 'What you been doin', suh – makin san' pies?'. The child is described as 'du'ty' (line 4), covered in syrupy 'merlasses' (line 5). However, the father compares the boy's dirtiness to his own in line 4 (a dirt we imagine gathered from hard work and labour in the fields – 'you's es du'ty ez me'). It continues as a quaint, domestic scene as the father**

> seeks help with the child, from his wife, the boy's mother, 'Maria' (line 6). But rather than being angry, the tone is merry, and the child is described in positive-sounding sibilant terms: all 'spa'klin eyes' (line 1) and 'so sticky and sweet' (line 8).
>
> In complete contrast to this light-hearted scene, Jonson's poem starts with a formal valedictory address: 'Farewell' (line 1), suggesting the distance between himself and his dead son, a contrasting image to the physical closeness we encounter in Dunbar's opening stanza. However, we do find Jonson paying a wonderful compliment to his lost son, describing the child as being 'of [his] right hand, and joy' (line 1), just like Dunbar's speaker who opens the poem with the affectionate term: 'Little brown baby wif spa'klin' eyes' (line 1). There is brightness in both images – the 'joy' of Jonson's boy and the sparkle in the eye of Dunbar's speaker's son. Poignantly, however, the opening of Jonson's poem goes on to state the age of his son as 'seven years' (line 3) and the moving image of the 'lov'd boy' (line 2) being 'lent' (line 3) to him, suggests the impermanence of the father's possession of his son, highlighting the brevity of their relationship together. Jonson intimately confesses that his 'sin was too much hope' (line 2) for his son, with their prospects and future being taken from them so soon. Overall then, in the openings of both poems we feel a sense of the fathers' separate prides, but see too how Dunbar's father figure revels in a closeness with his son, while Jonson laments the physical distance which has severed him from his boy.

As we see here, this running commentary of the opening of each poem has already established some points of comparison and contrast. What we need to do as we proceed with our analysis is to find patterns forming in the poems and further points of difference as we go.

Let's look again at the middle stanzas of Dunbar's poem and observe how the ideas develop:

> Little brown baby wif spa'klin' eyes,
> 10   Who's pappy's darlin' an' who's pappy's chile?
> Who is it all de day nevah once tries
> Fu' to be cross, er once loses dat smile?
> Whah did you git dem teef? My, you's a scamp!
> Whah did dat dimple come f'om in yo' chin?
> 15   Pappy do' know you—I b'lieves you's a tramp;
> Mammy, dis hyeah's some ol' straggler got in!

118   *Comparing Poems*

    Let's th'ow him outen de do' in de san',
    We do' want stragglers a-layin' 'roun' hyeah;
    Let's gin him 'way to de big buggah-man;
20 I know he's hidin' erroun' hyeah right neah.
    Buggah-man, buggah-man, come in de do',
    Hyeah's a bad boy you kin have fu' to eat.
    Mammy an' pappy do' want him no mo',
    Swaller him down f'om his haid to his feet!

Now, let's reread Jonson's middle lines, lines 5 to 8:

5 O, could I lose all father now! For why
    Will man lament the state he should envy?
    To have so soon 'scap'd world's and flesh's rage,
    And if no other misery, yet age?

> **Now as Dunbar's poem develops, the playfulness of the father really comes through. Stanza 2 and stanza 3 show how the father, the self-professed 'Pappy' (line 10) pretends not to know his dirty boy and threatens him with the frightening bogey man or 'buggah man' (line 19). The father lulls the unwitting son by charming him at first, asking: 'Who's pappy's darlin' and 'who's pappy's chile?' (line 10), before a shift in tone arrives, and the father exclaims: 'My, you's a scamp!' (line 13), calling once more to his wife, and jokingly pointing at his wide-eyed boy, shouting: 'Mammy, dis hyeah's some ol' straggler got in!' (line 16). The mocking irony is clear to the reader – we know it is a game – but the poor innocent boy, however, does not. The mock-sinister tone of the father arrives in the incantatory repetition of the ominous name: 'buggah-man' (line 19) – the mythical bogeyman child-catcher whom the father pretends he will summon to eat the boy ('swaller him down' on line 24), because 'Mammy an' pappy do' want him no mo' (line 23). In such a lively and spirited scene, we feel the joy of the father in his teasing here.**
>
>   **However, to turn to Jonson's poem at this stage shows us further the stark contrast in tones between the two pieces. Where Dunbar's father figure revels in the company of his boy and the possibility for jokes and light-hearted fun, Jonson shows us greater depths to the despair of the grieving father. Jonson's also uses exclamation, like Dunbar, but his tones on line 5 ('O, could I lose all father now!') are despondent. The feelings of loss are explicit and turn**

Comparing Poems 119

> into a philosophical contemplation, as it appears that Jonson seeks some solace, desperately, from somewhere. He questions why he should not 'envy' (line 6) his boy in death, ultimately reasoning that his seven-year-old has in fact avoided all suffering of the kind he feels as a father now: that his son, by dying young, has 'so soon 'scaped world's and flesh's rage' (line 7), and ultimately has avoided the inevitable 'misery' (line 8) and decay of old age. We question how much comfort this would really bring any parent here – the unconvincing rhetorical questions, exaggerate the father's woe further and paint a desperate figure overall.

As we come to the concluding phases of each poem, we should now seek further points of comparison or contrast.

Here is Dunbar's final stanza:

25 Dah, now, I t'ought dat you'd hug me up close.
     Go back, ol' buggah, you sha'n't have dis boy.
     He ain't no tramp, ner no straggler, of co'se;
     He's pappy's pa'dner an' play-mate an' joy.
     Come to you' pallet now — go to yo' res';
30 Wisht you could allus know ease an' cleah skies;
     Wisht you could stay jes' a chile on my breas'—
     Little brown baby wif spa'klin' eyes!

Now, let's look at the close of Jonson's poem:

     Rest in soft peace, and, ask'd, say, "Here doth lie
10 Ben Jonson his best piece of poetry."
     For whose sake henceforth all his vows be such,
     As what he loves may never like too much.

Here is a commentary of the closing phases:

> If we move away from the pity of Jonson's poem, and turn back to Dunbar's 'Little Brown Baby', the final stanza is one of true happiness and harmony. As noted before, the poem is a vivid, dramatic scene and in these final lines the father reveals the plan behind the teasing of his boy in the middle stanzas – it is all to earn a warm

embrace from his son: 'Dah, now, I t'ought dat you'd hug me up close' (line 25). It is a picture of father–son unity, and the father becomes exaggeratedly protective as he fends away the monster ('Go back, ol' buggah' on line 26) from ever snatching his son. The most moving line of the poem arrives on line 28, and shows how doting the father is. Hugging his son to him, the father states: 'He's pappy's pa'dner an' play-mate an' joy'. This line is most reminiscent of Jonson's fond opening statement in 'On My First Son'. For Dunbar's speaker too, his son is quite simply his 'joy'. The possessive, brightly alliterative 'Pappy's pa'dner an' playmate', is a similar image of father–son unity to Jonson's 'thou child of my right hand'. And it could be argued that 'Playmate' is perhaps the perfect way to summarise the nature of the father in Dunbar's poem overall. The last four lines of Dunbar's poem show the father in more serious mood, however. The sincere protectiveness rings out in the father's repetitive wish for his son to be always innocent and carefree, to 'allus know ease and cleah skies' (line 30) to stay 'jes 'a chile' on his 'breas'' (line 31). The last image of Dunbar's poem is of the father laying his son to bed, gently instructing for the boy to 'go to yo' res'' (line 29).

Interestingly, this image of sleep is echoed in the final lines of Jonson's poem. However, the sleep is of a different nature, being the sleep of death. Regardless, Jonson similarly urges for the child to 'Rest in soft peace' (line 9), before he builds to the greatest compliment possible for his son. As an epitaph for his boy, Jonson vividly imagines the headstone with the inscription: 'Here doth lie / Ben Jonson his best piece of poetry' (line 10). The great poet places all of his creative works, his entire written art, the poetry and the plays, below the creation of his boy. The superlative 'best' rings out with a heavy alliterative stress and assonantal echo of his own name 'Ben'. However, in final contrast to the easeful, contented father figure in Dunbar's 'Little Brown Baby', the focus with Jonson is on the lasting future unhappiness which awaits the grief-stricken father, as a man that from 'henceforth' (line 11) promises to never love in the same way, with the same intensity again: 'As what he loves may never like too much' (line 12).

At this stage in the study of the two poems we should find that a number of interesting points of contrast and comparison have emerged. It is now our job to write a meaningful conclusion which summarises and brings the two poems back into focus simultaneously. The conclusion is also a good opportunity to consider further the writers' methods and possible intentions. We should continue to work with the 'both–but' statements here, as a way of keeping the poems' similarities and differences clearly in mind.

> **In conclusion, we see that both poets, Dunbar and Jonson, present moving descriptions of the father figures in the two poems. Both choose a fitting tone for the situation of their poems too. The dialect language of Dunbar immediately achieves a fond, playful, intimate nature in the father-speaker of 'Little Brown Baby', whereas the high, formal tones of Jonson show the greatest respect for his 'lov'd boy' (line 2). Both poems are vivid in their presentation of the father's protectiveness and pride – with the most revealing commonality being that, in life or death, both sons remain the 'joy' in their father's lives. What we see with powerful poetry of this kind is an ability to describe the universal bond of father and sons, even though the poets are from entirely different time periods and cultures.**

As noted on previous examples, if you would like to gain greater understanding of how the structure of the 5-part essay works, now would be a good time to read over the essay in full without the interrupting notes in between. Simply go back and read through the paragraphs in bold to achieve this.

Practice

As we have seen, there is a lot to juggle when comparing two poems together, and in order to create a suitable balance between the poems we need to have a careful structure for our points – the 5-part essay, enables us to do this effectively and to think in quite a sophisticated way at times.

The important thing to remember when conducting a comparison between two poems is the timing of the comparison comments. We see, in both example essays, a need for clear comparison and contrast statements at different times throughout, particularly when we move from comments about one poem to the next. This enables us to keep both poems in mind constantly and to maintain a clear line of argument.

Therefore, be alert to phrases and transition statements (often referred to as discourse markers), such as: 'both', 'similarly', 'in comparison', 'in contrast', 'contrastingly', 'but', 'instead', and 'however' (to name but a few). Using such terms naturally and frequently will result in a strong style.

Note also, that the introduction and conclusion are opportunities for clear comparison too.

The introduction treats both poems simultaneously in a brief summary style around the given theme from the question; however, the conclusion is an opportunity to revaluate and consider all manner of similarities and differences in a meaningful way at the end of the study overall.

Now is a good time to practise.

In the following pages, we have four comparison questions and eight poems.

Compare how the poets Anna Wickham (1883–1947) and Sarojini Naidu (1879–1949) <u>celebrate motherhood</u> in their respective poems, 'After Annunciation' and 'Cradle Song'.

After Annunciation

by Anna Wickham

    Rest, little Guest,
    Beneath my breast.
    Feed, sweet Seed,
    At your need.
5   I took Love for my lord
    And this is my reward,
    My body is good earth,
    That you, dear Plant, have birth.

Cradle Song

by Sarojini Naidu

    From groves of spice,
    O'er fields of rice,
    Athwart the lotus-stream,
    I bring for you,
5   Aglint with dew,
    A little lovely dream.

    Sweet, shut your eyes,
    The wild fire-flies
    Dance through the fairy neem;
    From the poppy-bole
10 For you I stole
    A little lovely dream.

    Dear eyes, good night,
    In golden light
    The stars around you gleam;

15 On you I Press
    With soft caress
    A little lovely dream.

Compare how Edmund Spenser (1553–1599) and William Shakespeare (1564–1616) present ideas of <u>enduring love</u> in the poems 'One day I wrote her name upon the strand' and 'Sonnet 18'.

One day I wrote her name upon the strand

by Edmund Spenser

    One day I wrote her name upon the strand,
    But came the waves and washed it away:
    Again I wrote it with a second hand,
    But came the tide, and made my pains his prey.
5 "Vain man," said she, "that dost in vain assay,
    A mortal thing so to immortalize;
    For I myself shall like to this decay,
    And eke my name be wiped out likewise."
    "Not so," (quod I) "let baser things devise
10 To die in dust, but you shall live by fame:
    My verse your vertues rare shall eternize,
    And in the heavens write your glorious name:
    Where whenas death shall all the world subdue,
    Our love shall live, and later life renew."

Sonnet 18

by William Shakespeare

    Shall I compare thee to a summer's day?
    Thou art more lovely and more temperate:
    Rough winds do shake the darling buds of May,
    And summer's lease hath all too short a date;
5 Sometime too hot the eye of heaven shines,
    And often is his gold complexion dimm'd;
    And every fair from fair sometime declines,
    By chance or nature's changing course untrimm'd;
    But thy eternal summer shall not fade,
10 Nor lose possession of that fair thou ow'st;
    Nor shall death brag thou wander'st in his shade,
    When in eternal lines to time thou grow'st:
       So long as men can breathe or eyes can see,
       So long lives this, and this gives life to thee.

Compare how Charlotte Mew (1869–1928) and Anne Bradstreet (1612–1672) describe <u>intimate relationships</u> in the poems 'Rooms' and 'To My Dear and Loving Husband'.

Rooms

by Charlotte Mew

    I remember rooms that have had their part
      In the steady slowing down of the heart.
    The room in Paris, the room at Geneva,
    The little damp room with the seaweed smell,
5   And that ceaseless maddening sound of the tide—
      Rooms where for good or for ill—things died.
    But there is the room where we (two) lie dead,
    Though every morning we seem to wake and might just as well seem to sleep again
      As we shall somewhere in the other quieter, dustier bed
10 Out there in the sun—in the rain.

To My Dear and Loving Husband

by Anne Bradstreet

    If ever two were one, then surely we.
    If ever man were loved by wife, then thee.
    If ever wife was happy in a man,
    Compare with me, ye women, if you can.
5   I prize thy love more than whole mines of gold,
    Or all the riches that the East doth hold.
    My love is such that rivers cannot quench,
    Nor ought but love from thee give recompense.
    Thy love is such I can no way repay;
10 The heavens reward thee manifold, I pray.
    Then while we live, in love let's so persever,
    That when we live no more, we may live ever.

Compare how John Keats (1795–1821) and Violet Jacob (1863–1946) describe <u>the landscape</u> in their respective poems, 'To Ailsa Rock' and 'Craigo Woods'.

To Ailsa Rock

by John Keats

    Hearken, thou craggy ocean pyramid!
    Give answer from thy voice – the sea-fowl's screams!

When were thy shoulders mantled in huge streams?
When from the sun was thy broad forehead hid?
5 How long is't since the mighty Power bid
Thee heave to airy sleep from fathom dreams –
Sleep in the lap of thunder or sunbeams –
Or when gray clouds are thy cold coverlid?
Thou answerest not, for thou art dead asleep.
10 Thy life is but two dead eternities –
The last in air, the former in the deep!
First with the whales, last with the eagle skies!
Drown'd wast thou till an earthquake made thee steep,
Another cannot wake thy giant size!

Craigo Woods

by Violet Jacob

Craigo Woods, wi' the splash o' the cauld rain beatin'
I' the back end o' the year,
When the clouds hang laigh wi' the weicht o' their load o' greetin'
And the autumn wind's asteer;
5 Ye may stand like gaists, ye may fa' i' the blast that's cleft ye
To rot i' the chilly dew,
But when will I mind on aucht since the day I left ye
Like I mind on you – on you?

Craigo Woods, i' the licht o' September sleepin'
10 And the saft mist o' the morn,
When the hairst climbs to yer feet, an' the sound o' reapin'
Comes up frae the stookit corn,
And the braw reid puddock-stules are like jewels blinkin'
And the bramble happs ye baith,
15 O what do I see, i' the lang nicht, lyin' an' thinkin'
As I see yer wraith – yer wraith?

There's a road to a far-aff land, an' the land is yonder
Whaur a' men's hopes are set;
We dinna ken foo lang we maun hae to wander,
20 But we'll a' win to it yet;
An' gin there's woods o' fir an' the licht atween them,
I winna speir its name,
But I'll lay me doon by the puddock-stules when I've seen them,
An' I'll cry "I'm hame – I'm hame!"

8 Exploring a Group of Poems

In this final chapter, we are going to attempt something quite challenging. We are going to explore four poems by a single poet and use our notes to write an essay which discusses the writer's work in general.

Learning a number of pieces by a single poet and becoming more familiar with a poet's general themes and style is something we see university students doing widely – it is also something that the general lover of poetry does too (although they may not necessarily think to write their thoughts down on paper in the form of an essay).

For example, if we are studying a particular poet or have a favourite writer, it is likely that we will have read a number of their works, and so, in conversation we might be able to mention and comment on a range of different poems which might strike us as memorable or relevant to the discussion.

This quite natural, conversational style is essentially what we will try to do when examining a group of poems by a single poet in an essay. However, we will need to think carefully about how we make our points and observations, and how we construct our thoughts clearly on the page.

Once more, for this type of essay we can adopt the 5-part essay method. By using this, we can write a clear introduction which briefly introduces the four poems; we can then explore three key themes in the main body of the essay, before making a conclusion about our findings.

The first thing we must do, though, is to read the four poems carefully, to summarise each succinctly, and then to look for patterns and trends which are occurring throughout the poet's work. This will enable us to choose the three key themes upon which we will build our essay.

For the first study, we are going to look at four poems by the nature poet, John Clare (1793–1864). Take your time to read and enjoy each one:

Open Winter

by John Clare

> Where slanting banks are always with the sun
> The daisy is in blossom even now;

      And where warm patches by the hedges run
      The cottager when coming home from plough
5   Brings home a cowslip root in flower to set.
      Thus ere the Christmas goes the spring is met
      Setting up little tents about the fields
      In sheltered spots. – Primroses when they get
      Behind the wood's old roots, where ivy shields
10 Their crimpled, curdled leaves, will shine and hide.
      Cart ruts and horses' footings scarcely yield
      A slur for boys, just crizzled and that's all.
      Frost shoots his needles by the small dyke side,
      And snow in scarce a feather's seen to fall.

Birds at Evening

by John Clare

      I love to hear the evening crows go by
      And see the starnels darken down the sky.
      The bleaching stack the bustling sparrow leaves
      And plops with merry note beneath the eaves.
5   The odd and lated pigeon bounces by
      As if a wary watching hawk was nigh,
      While far and fearing nothing, high and slow,
      The stranger birds to distant places go,
      While short of flight the evening robin comes
10 To watch the maiden sweeping out the crumbs
      Nor fears the idle shout of passing boy
      But pecks about the door and sings for joy;
      Then in the hovel where the cows are fed
      Finds till the morning comes a pleasant bed.

To the Fox Fern

by John Clare

      Haunter of woods, lone wilds and solitudes
      Where none but feet of birds and things as wild
      Doth print a foot track near, where summer's light
      Buried in boughs forgets its glare and round thy crimpèd leaves
5   Feints in a quiet dimness fit for musings
      And melancholy moods, with here and there
      A golden thread of sunshine stealing through

The evening shadowy leaves that seem to creep
Like leisure in the shade.

Summer

by John Clare

Come we to the summer, to the summer we will come,
For the woods are full of bluebells and the hedges full of bloom,
And the crow is on the oak a-building of her nest,
And love is burning diamonds in my true lover's breast;
5   She sits beneath the whitethorn a-plaiting of her hair,
And I will to my true lover with a fond request repair;
I will look upon her face, I will in her beauty rest,
And lay my aching weariness upon her lovely breast.

The clock-a-clay is creeping on the open bloom of May,
10 The merry bee is trampling the pinky threads all day,
And the chaffinch it is brooding on its grey mossy nest
In the whitethorn bush where I will lean upon my lover's breast;
I'll lean upon her breast and I'll whisper in her ear
That I cannot get a wink o'sleep for thinking of my dear;
15 I hunger at my meat and I daily fade away
Like the hedge rose that is broken in the heat of the day.

To start with, after first reading, it is worth briefly summarising each poem and considering some of the key themes in each one. Here are my notes:

- 'Open Winter' is a sonnet which considers the seasons, particularly the change from winter to spring. In this poem, Clare writes of a cottager and some playful boys, so we get an important human element to this poem.
- 'Birds at Evening' is another sonnet which has a joyful tone and celebrates bird-life from the speaker's perspective. It is full of positive, **pastoral** descriptions.
- 'To the Fox Fern' is an interesting lyric poem. It is short and precise, quite philosophical, and uses the plant (the fox fern) to prompt the poet's musings.
- 'Summer' is another seasonal poem which shows how nature forms the fitting backdrop for love and romance. Once more it is a celebration of the beauty of the natural world and very precise in its close details.

So, after these short summaries, we are beginning to get a 'feel' for John Clare's poetry. It appears that Clare is keen to celebrate the beauty of the natural world, he has an obvious appreciation for the close details and descriptions in his poems of bird, bug, plant, and human life, after all.

Therefore, with this preliminary detective work in mind, we are now in a position to begin developing our essay. Here is the title:

Explore some of the ways in which John Clare presents <u>the natural world</u> in his poems.

Right, let's go!

We want to consider all four poems now and to decide on three key themes to form the body of the essay. We should look for the general patterns and ideas which arise across the poems in order to do this. And, after reviewing the summaries of each poem above, it seems as if we can limit our study to these shared themes: the seasons, birds, and human beings.

This means that we can focus on some of Clare's descriptive, atmospheric writing in his observations of Winter, Spring, and Summer; then we can examine his interest in birdlife, and finally we can explore how he shows human interaction with the natural world in his poems too. This will make for a comprehensive study.

Overall then, we will construct our 5-part essay along these lines:

- Introduction
- Seasons
- Birds
- Human Beings
- Conclusion

We begin, as always, with a summary introduction, outlining the poems in general:

> **In his work, John Clare presents a rich portrait of the natural world. He keenly explores the interactions between human beings and nature too, evincing very intimate and personal tones at times. He shows how changing seasons evoke different human emotions in poems like 'Open Winter' and 'Summer', while his appreciation of both native and migratory birdlife is evident in a poem like 'Birds at Evening'. Close observations of nature are also definitive of his style and we see how the mere sighting of a plant in 'To a Fox Fern' can inspire his own philosophical musings too.**

Again, this introduction is written to around 100 words, in keeping with the essays we have attempted in the previous sections. It is a bit of a challenge to keep four poems in mind in a short space of time, but it can be done with some careful consideration and skill. The main purpose of this introduction is to set up the essay and give the reader some sense of what is to come in the body of the piece.

Exploring a Group of Poems

If we turn back to our plan, we wanted to discuss the seasons, birds, and human beings in the work of John Clare, so let's work in that order and open the essay with a discussion on the seasons. To create a nice range of points we should refer to as many poems as are relevant from the collection – if all four apply, then we should mention them all at some stage. If only two or three apply, then only mention those. Again, we should write naturally and convincingly and not force an argument that simply isn't there.

So, we should now return to each poem in the collection, reading with the first key theme, 'the seasons', in mind. Any relevant references should be noted down for possible inclusion in the essay.

Here are some initial notes on the seasons in the four poems:

In 'Open Winter' the harshness of the winter season comes through starkly in contrast to the more delicate descriptions of spring. 'Birds at Evening' does not really address the seasons explicitly; however, there does appear to be an interesting reference to migrating birds ('the stranger birds to distant places go') which could be used in this section. 'To the Fox Fern' is a bright, summer poem, describing images of light throughout. 'In Summer' uses the summer season as a backdrop for the high romance of the scene described.

Here's an attempt then at the first section of the essay, trying to include some of the observations above in a more formal style:

> **One notable feature of Clare's nature writing is his interest in time and the interrelationship between the seasons. Clare is aware of the hardship of winter, yet still shows how a beauty in the landscape itself remains. In 'Open Winter' for example, he describes how aggressive the season can be, personifying the cold weather as a 'Frost' which 'shoots his needles' (line 13) into the ditches and dykes of the land, while the cart tracks and horse hoofs leave the cold earth in a churned and spiky, 'crizzled' (line 12) state. Yet, he holds onto the positive signs, even in the deathly season. The speaker in 'Open Winter' is joyful, exclaiming how the 'daisy is in blossom even now' (line 2), observing how the ivy 'shields' (line 9) and protects the pretty primroses (flowers of the coming spring) which 'shine and hide' (line 10) behind them. And spring appears to be a blessing for Clare. There is a feeling in 'Open Winter' that the waiting will soon be over and that the new season is already setting up camp 'in little tents about the fields' (line 7) of winter, ready to take over the landscape when the time is right. This is a playful metaphor for the changing seasons, which sets the mood for the entire poem.**

> This sense of excitement at the arrival of a new season is also evident in his poems about summer. 'To the Fox Fern' shows how the blessed 'summer's light' (line 3) is languid and joyous, 'forgets' even its own 'glare' (line 4), and plays shadow games and 'feints' (line 5), passing across the fronds of the fox fern plant. Once more, Clare's act of personification imbues nature with life, culminating in the praising metaphor, which likens the summer light to 'a golden thread of sunshine' (line 7). However, it is in the poem which is dedicated to the season itself, 'Summer', where we learn of Clare's true appreciation for this time of year. The opening line of the poem reads like an incantation, as if the speaker and his lover are magnetically drawn to the season: 'Come we to the summer, to the summer we will come' (line 1). The caesura creates a powerful pause before we hear the spell-like echo of the word 'come' again. In 'Summer' the whole scenic landscape becomes a backdrop for the central couple, the romantic speaker who will 'rest' (line 7) upon the 'lovely breast' (line 8) of his mistress under the idyllic whitethorn tree. All the while, in this harmonious scene, Clare observes the fine details of the abundant season: 'the woods full of bluebells and the hedges full of bloom' (line 2), the tiny ladybird (the 'clock-a-clay' of line 9) and the 'merry bee' (line 10) among the 'pinky threads' (line 10) of flowers. The scene is joyous and teeming with vitality and the 'heat of the day' (line 16).

Now, we should turn our thoughts to the next section of the essay and Clare's descriptions of birds in his poems. Once more, we must revisit each poem, reading each one for the second key theme: 'birds'. We should note any relevant references for possible inclusion in the essay.

Here are some notes:

'Open Winter' is not really a bird poem and has no explicit descriptions; therefore, it will not factor into this section of the essay. This is not a problem because we have already devoted some attention to this poem in the seasons section. 'Birds at Evening' is the main poem in this section (this is also important because it did not feature in the seasons section). We see a great listing of different species of birds and the speaker's obvious love of birds throughout. 'To the Fox Fern' makes an interesting, subtle reference to birds in line 2 (solitudes / Where none but feet of birds and things as wild / Doth print a foot track near) to show the general absence of activity from the overall still and silent scene described in the poem. 'In Summer' is another main bird poem which utilises personification to great effect, as Clare reimagines bird behaviours for the reader in this human way.

Here then, is an attempt at turning these general notes into stronger, formal essay analysis. Remember, that we are trying to build this section about 'birds' upon the first section about 'the seasons'. Note the important word 'too' in the opening sentence of the paragraph which follows – this is the linking word which gives a sense of structure between the sections here:

> **In the poem 'Birds at Evening', Clare uses the sonnet form to celebrate all manner of birdlife too. His speaker opens with an impassioned declaration: 'I love to hear the evening crows go by…' (line 1) before proceeding to list a host of different native birds throughout the rest of the poem. We hear of 'starnels' (line 2), which is Clare's colloquial term for starlings, and energetic, 'bustling sparrows' (line 3) who are 'merry' (line 4) in their movements. Clare even contrasts the prosaic 'odd and lated pigeon' (line 5) with the majestically 'watching hawk' (line 6), to show his universal appreciation of the common and not so common birds he observes. Clare sweeps on and refers to the migratory birds in the second half of the poem ('the stranger birds to distant places go' on line 8), before he closes the poem with a final and lasting focus on the 'evening robin' (line 10), self-assured and singing 'for joy' (line 12), which makes its 'pleasant bed' (line 14) in the cattle stalls.**
>
> **We find also that birds appear in some form or another in several of his other poems. In 'To the Fox Fern', Clare establishes a quiet woodland scene, playing with light and shadow, to give a general elusiveness to the poem. The poem itself is short and elusive too, with Clare creating a distinct lack of action and activity throughout; the only marks of life being the faint 'feet of birds' (line 3) left in the tracks of the ground. Also in 'Summer', Clare further injects different birds with life, personifying them at times. His industrious 'crow is on the oak a-building of her nest' (line 3), while the calm and pensive chaffinch in the second stanza of the poem is 'brooding on its grey mossy nest' (line 11). In both images we see acts of deliberate and careful nesting, as the diligent birds prepare their homes, harmoniously in the summer months.**

Having discussed a good range of relevant points across three of the four poems in this second section, we can now move on to the third key theme – humans.

Once more, the method is the same. We must reread each poem with a focus on 'humans', noting any relevant references which could appear in the essay itself.

Here are some general notes:

'Open Winter' includes explicit reference to different human beings: 'the lowly cottager' and the playful 'boys'. Both are seen interacting with nature – the cottager who ploughs the fields and appreciates the beauty of a single flower, and the boys who are seen playing wildly outside. 'Birds at Evening' employs an admiring human speaker who describes the interplay between human beings and birds to imaginative effect. 'To A Fox Fern' is unique in Clare trying to capture a complete absence of human life in the natural landscape he describes. Finally, 'Summer' is very important for this section as the human couple are central to the action of the poem, as they find love and romance in picturesque, natural surroundings.

From these general observations, here is a more detailed, cohesive commentary. Note how we try to tie the sections of the essay together seamlessly. As the last point mentioned in the section on birds was about 'harmony', so the starting point in this section is about 'harmony' too. Therefore 'To A Fox Fern' is the first poem explored:

> **And it is this idea of harmony that is key to Clare's poetry overall, particularly when we view the interactions between the human world and the natural world itself. For example, as seen in 'To the Fox Fern', Clare focuses on the absence of human life entirely to show us the 'quiet dimness fit for musings / And melancholy moods' (lines 5 to 6) which is found in the natural world, demonstrating how nature inspires us to think deeply and emotionally, even affecting our moods accordingly. Clare's solitary speaker, coming upon the solitude of the woods, feels this profoundly. We see this idea once more in 'Birds at Evening' where the interaction between human beings and the natural world is quite symbiotic – evident in the figure of the patient robin who waits to feed, watching calmly the maiden 'sweeping out the crumbs' (line 10), and who does not fear the 'idle shout of passing boys' (line 11), such is its tameness and being used to human contact.**
>
> **As noted, in the poem 'Summer', Clare uses the natural world as a fitting setting for the romantic couple of the speaker and mistress, who both lay down under the shade of a tree while surrounded by an array of pretty plant, bird, and animal life. Clare uses a very evocative rhyme in the second stanza of this poem of 'nest' (line 11) and 'breast' (line 12) to show the speaker's sense of being attuned with nature, drawing parallels between the snug nesting place of the chaffinch and the soft bosom of his mistress: 'And the chaffinch in its brooding on its grey mossy nest / In the whitethorn bush where**

134   *Exploring a Group of Poems*

> **I will lean upon my lover's breast' (lines 12 to 13). Clare ends the poem further highlighting the kinship that the speaker shares with nature in the simile: 'I daily fade away / Like the hedge rose that is broken in the heat of day' (lines 15 to 16), perhaps suggesting the speaker's being entirely worn out by his own overwhelming passion on such a romantic outing. A more quaint, less sensual, image of humanity's attachment to nature, however, is seen in one of the opening images in 'Open Winter' where the lowly cottager, after a hard day's working in the fields, 'Brings home a cowslip root in flower to set' (line 5). This image sums up Clare's sentiments really, in the humble figure of the worker who seeks to become closer to the natural world by instinctively possessing a piece of it for himself – in what is a very human gesture, after all.**

We are now in a position to evaluate what we have found, and make a meaningful conclusion. Here, it is important to address each of the poems in the study separately in its own right, before noting the overall patterns and trends across the collection:

> **Overall, we find that Clare often romanticises the natural world in his poems. We find in poems like 'Summer' the landscape becomes a backdrop for human action, for love and harmony of spirit. Whereas in 'To the Fox Fern', a brief moment in time in the silent, deserted woods is the focus for Clare, with a distinct lack of human life the key to the solitude of the scene. We also discover that Clare often echoes descriptions of human behaviour in his descriptions of nature, and how in poems like 'Birds at Evening' his deliberate and instinctive acts of personification enliven the scene and make familiar, common birds more familiar to us somehow. Ultimately, this is achieved by the closest attention to detail and observation of the natural world. Be it the almost imperceptible signs in the changing seasons that we see in 'Open Winter', microscopic bug life, exotic plant life, or the often prosaic birdlife around us – things we modern folk might take for granted – Clare somehow magnifies it all, casting his own lens over it, to expose some of the magic and wonder he finds hidden within.**

As noted before, a good habit at this stage is to go back through this section on John Clare and to read only the formal essay paragraphs (you can find these in bold font). By ignoring the interrupting notes, you will be better able to follow the structure of the essay and the more complex line of argument that occurs.

Getting a strong sense of how you can recreate an essay structure of this kind will be extremely beneficial, particularly when you are faced with a group of poems in this way.

To consolidate this, however, we can start by looking at another group of poems by the brilliant Emily Brontë (1818–48), best known for her novel *Wuthering Heights*.

We will examine four of her poems and attempt to answer the following question:

How does Emily Brontë present <u>the speaker</u> in her poems?

This time, as you read, try to be alert to any big themes, general patterns or ideas which form across the collection. You might even want to write down some of your observations as you go.

Spellbound

by Emily Brontë

> The night is darkening round me,
> The wild winds coldly blow;
> But a tyrant spell has bound me
> And I cannot, cannot go.
>
> 5   The giant trees are bending
> Their bare boughs weighed with snow.
> And the storm is fast descending,
> And yet I cannot go.
>
> Clouds beyond clouds above me,
> 10 Wastes beyond wastes below;
> But nothing drear can move me;
> I will not, cannot go.

The Visionary

by Emily Brontë

> Silent is the house: all are laid asleep:
> One alone looks out o'er the snow-wreaths deep,
> Watching every cloud, dreading every breeze
> That whirls the wildering drift, and bends the groaning trees.

5   Cheerful is the hearth, soft the matted floor;
    Not one shivering gust creeps through pane or door;
    The little lamp burns straight, its rays shoot strong and far:
    I trim it well, to be the wanderer's guiding-star.

    Frown, my haughty sire! chide, my angry dame!
10 Set your slaves to spy; threaten me with shame:
    But neither sire nor dame nor prying serf shall know,
    What angel nightly tracks that waste of frozen snow.

    What I love shall come like visitant of air,
    Safe in secret power from lurking human snare;
15 What loves me, no word of mine shall e'er betray,
    Though for faith unstained my life must forfeit pay.

    Burn, then, little lamp; glimmer straight and clear—
    Hush! a rustling wing stirs, methinks, the air:
    He for whom I wait, thus ever comes to me;
20 Strange Power! I trust thy might; trust thou my constancy.

I Am the Only Being Whose Doom

by Emily Brontë

   I am the only being whose doom
   No tongue would ask, no eye would mourn;
   I never caused a thought of gloom,
   A smile of joy, since I was born.

5 In secret pleasure, secret tears,
   This changeful life has slipped away,
   As friendless after eighteen years,
   As lone as on my natal day.

   There have been times I cannot hide,
10 There have been times when this was drear,
   When my sad soul forgot its pride
   And longed for one to love me here.

   But those were in the early glow
   Of feelings since subdued by care;
15 And they have died so long ago,
   I hardly now believe they were.

First melted off the hope of youth,
Then fancy's rainbow fast withdrew;
And then experience told me truth
20 In mortal bosoms never grew.

'Twas grief enough to think mankind
All hollow, servile, insincere;
But worse to trust to my own mind
And find the same corruption there.

Long Neglect Has Worn Away

by Emily Brontë

Long neglect has worn away
Half the sweet enchanting smile;
Time has turned the bloom to grey;
Mould and damp the face defile.

5   But that lock of silky hair,
Still beneath the picture twined,
Tells what once those features were,
Paints their image on the mind.

Fair the hand that traced that line,
10 "Dearest, ever deem me true";
Swiftly flew the fingers fine
When the pen that motto drew.

In order to prepare for this essay, 'How does Brontë present the speaker in her poems?', it is important once more to think of each poem separately first and to provide brief summaries. This will enable us to identify patterns or commonalities in the poems, which will then help us form the three main sections for the essay itself.

Here are the summaries:

- In 'Spellbound' we meet a first-person speaker who is feeling trapped and isolated. The setting of the poem is at night and the scene is one of a cold winter. We read of a 'spell' that stifles the speaker and see how affected she is by the surrounding landscape. The refrain is effective in repeating the idea that the speaker 'cannot go'.
- 'The Visionary' is another poem which reveals an isolated first-person speaker. It reads like a dramatic monologue, or a stream of consciousness, as the speaker, alone in her room, away from her overbearing parents,

holds up a candle in the hope of directing a mysterious figure – the 'He for whom I wait' – to her. Once more, the elements play a significant part – the wind and the snow are key.
- 'I Am the Only Being Whose Doom' is a bleak presentation of a solitary speaker, suffering from feelings of loneliness and being unloved. There is a great hopelessness in this poem and a sense of innocence to painful experience, of self-criticism and self-doubt. It is very much a raw, confessional poem.
- 'Long Neglect Has Worn Away' is a piece which discusses time and the painful sense of love and parting. The speaker laments her own ageing and the period of separation from the lover described in the poem. The poem is a vivid, dramatic scene in which the speaker observes a portrait of the lost love and holds a lock of his hair. There is a sense that the lover left or died swiftly and the grief of the speaker is clear.

So, after a review of these summaries, it is quite clear that in each of the poems, Brontë is quick to establish her speaker as an isolated figure. Therefore, one of the important themes which we should discuss in the essay to come is 'isolation'.

Also, when scanning the summaries, it seems Brontë often establishes a romantic connection between the speaker and an unnamed addressee. This is evident in two poems mainly: 'The Visionary' and 'Long Neglect Has Worn Away'. In each example there is some uncertainty or vulnerability in the speaker, and this is also the more general theme, which will help us factor in the two other poems into the discussion. Therefore, 'vulnerability' will be the second topic for the essay.

To finish, what might strike us as being interesting are the vivid scenes or settings which Brontë describes in her poetry. Therefore, we can explore how the confines of the locations and the elements themselves (notably the wind and the snow) impact on the speakers in each case. In light of this, we will then explore 'the impact of the setting on the speaker' as the third section of the essay.

Overall then, we will construct our 5-part essay along these lines:

- Introduction
- Isolation
- Vulnerability
- Settings
- Conclusion

Let's begin with a brief introduction which addresses the question and introduces the four studied poems. We want to write this to around 100 words:

It is clear that in Emily Brontë's poetry the first-person speaker is an important lens through which we see some of the more bleak

> aspects of human existence. Her poems often include vivid settings which impact on the speaker, and poems like 'The Visionary' and 'Long Neglect Has worn Away' describe some of the uncertainties and feelings which come with love and loss, while other poems like 'Spellbound' and 'I Am the Only Being Whose Doom' present grave ideas of solitude and the psychological impact of being isolated and left alone with dark and brooding thoughts.

From here, we are in a position to move on to the first point of the discussion – isolation. We want to create a balance between the four poems and factor all into the discussion, if possible. We want to look for similarities and points of difference. We need to be fairly fast-moving in our commentary, but know that it is important to quote from the poems when and where relevant.

In typical style, we must reread the poems now with 'isolation' in mind and look for possible references for the essay itself.

Here are some brief notes on isolation in each poem:

Isolation in 'Spellbound' is seen in how the speaker is alone in the wilds (with no human company), while only sky and waste surround. Important images are: 'Clouds beyond clouds above me' and 'Wastes beyond wastes below'. Next, isolation in 'The Visionary' is seen starkly in images like 'all are laid asleep' where Brontë manages to isolate the figure of the speaker, even though she is placed in company in the family home. 'Safe in secret power from lurking human snare' also suggests the speaker is mistrustful of other people, wills her own isolation, and longs to be with one person only. Moving on, isolation in 'I Am the Only Being Whose Doom' comes about because of being 'friendless'. The speaker is a young girl of 18 years, a figure who is mistrusting of human kind – the final stanza is key in revealing this. Finally, in 'Long Neglect Has Worn Away', isolation is seen mainly in the time references and the second stanza is most important in showing this. The isolation in this poem comes about because of a lost love. It is a poem of grief and longing for a return to the past.

Now, here is more formal essay commentary, based on these notes:

> When we think of the feelings of isolation which are evident in Brontë's poems, we should consider the fact that some of her speakers wilfully call on a sense of solitariness, while others have it forced upon them. There seems, in a poem like 'The Visionary', for example, a triumphant joy on the isolated speaker's part as she guides the mysterious figure ('He for whom I wait' on line 19) to her from the 'secret' (line 14) confines of her bedroom by aid of

torchlight. The speaker is wary of her overbearing (probably critical) parents – the 'sire' and the 'dame' on line 19 – and is mistrustful of how other people might spoil her romance, knowing that it is only 'safe in secret power from lurking human snare' (line 14). This general distrust of humanity (or feeling of misanthropy) which Brontë describes is seen further in a poem like 'I Am the Only Being Whose Doom' where the young, 18-year-old speaker, in a bleak, confessional monologue talks explicitly of being 'friendless' (line 7) and admits in the final stanza to thinking 'mankind / All hollow, servile, insincere' (lines 21 to 22).

Isolation takes on a different form in the speakers of poems like 'Spellbound' and 'Long Neglect Has Worn Away', however, as we see two interesting depictions of lost and lonely figures. In 'Spellbound' once more, we see Brontë describing a speaker who somehow has a perverse pleasure in her own solitude. The speaker is alone in the wilds with no human company, transfixed, seemingly swallowed up by the foreboding landscape. The refrain in the poem is most effective, repeating throughout: 'And I cannot, cannot go' (line 4); 'And yet I cannot go' (line 8); 'I will not, cannot go' (line 12). In contrast to this wilful isolation, in 'Long Neglect Has Worn Away', we meet a grieving speaker who is longing for a return to the past and pining for a lost love. In the present action of the poem, she looks on at two objects: a portrait of her love and a lock of his hair ('But that lock of silky hair, / Still beneath the picture twined' on lines 5 to 6). The poignant past tense verb 'were' in the following lines: 'Tells what once those features were / Paints their image on the mind' (lines 7 to 8) shows how it is memory of this kind that reminds the speaker of her loss and her unwanted isolation.

From here, we can turn our thoughts to the second key theme from our essay plan: 'vulnerability'. Again, we must reread the poems, making our notes on the relevant references which might help with the essay itself.

Here are some general observations, which we can then seek to turn into a more formal commentary:

Vulnerability is most evident in 'Spellbound' in the 'spell' or magic which seems to transfix the speaker here. We question whether it is a spell of the mind – a madness or perversion in the speaker – or whether it is the harsh, unforgiving landscape. Either way, the speaker cannot leave the scene and is subject to the wilds. Next, the vulnerability which occurs in 'The Visionary' is seen in the tension of the scene. We know that the speaker is involved in

Exploring a Group of Poems 141

an illicit love of some kind, and is nervously awaiting the arrival of her secret lover. The final stanza is key in revealing the speaker's own doubts, however, about whether or not the mysterious figure will arrive to meet her. Moving on, the vulnerability we see in 'I Am the Only Being Whose Doom' is most apparent in the extreme psychological isolation of the speaker. She is vulnerable because of her unflinching self-criticism – defined in the first and last stanzas explicitly. Finally, the vulnerability in 'Long Neglect Has Worn Away' is seen two-fold: first in the physical ageing and frailty of the speaker ('Time has turned the bloom to grey; / Mould and damp the face defile') and second in the speaker's reflection in the final stanza that the 'Fair hand' of her lost love 'Swiftly flew' in the act of writing loving terms to her, (but ironically has 'flown' because of his parting).

Here is the next section on vulnerability. We should note the importance of trying to build this section upon the previous section about 'isolation'. Our starting sentence for the following paragraph has a vital role in doing this – note here how both key words 'isolation' and 'vulnerability' are used:

> **Interestingly, Brontë shows how even those speakers who seem to desire isolation become very vulnerable. This is the case with the speaker in the poem 'Spellbound'. In many ways the poem is a psychological study of the wracked mind of the vulnerable speaker who is at the mercy of the wild landscape and caught in its transfixing 'tyrant spell' (line 3). The force of its effect works upon the speaker to the point where she even seems perversely to be emboldened, stating in the penultimate line: 'but nothing drear can move me' (line 11). Similarly, the speaker in 'The Visionary' is also caught between being emboldened and feeling vulnerable. The relationship which Brontë describes in this poem is an illicit one it seems, and the speaker waits excitedly, patiently, longingly for her forbidden love to emerge. The final stanza of the poem is most revealing about the speaker's nervous position, however, as she states: 'He for whom I wait, thus ever comes to me; / Strange Power! I trust thy might; trust thou my constancy' (lines 19 to 20). The vulnerability in this poem is heightened as there is a lingering question over who or what the mysterious figure is – he is described at different times as 'he' (line 19), as 'angel' (line 12), as 'strange power' (line 20). We are left to question whether the speaker is subject here to a human love or something entirely other. The repetition of the word 'trust' in the final line adds to this, implying a certain desperation, or a lingering hope. After all, the poem ends without our knowing if this strange figure ever actually arrives.**

> In terms of more stark examples of vulnerability, we find that both poems 'I Am the Only Being Whose Doom' and 'Long Neglect Has Worn Away' demonstrate suffering figures explicitly. The self-criticising speaker of 'I Am the Only Being Whose Doom', for example, is unflinching. In the opening stanza Brontë sets up this painfully-tortured voice, who claims from the outset that she is unloved and has left no emotional mark on the world: 'I am the only being whose doom / No tongue would ask, no eye would mourn' (lines 1 to 2). The extreme psychological isolation extends into the next lines: 'I never caused a thought of gloom, / A smile of joy, since I was born' (lines 3 to 4). The speaker essentially dismisses her entire existence as meaningless. The fact that the poem ends on the same critical viewpoint exaggerates the lasting vulnerability and frailty of the speaker. And so, after damning the rest of the corrupt humanity she turns the damnation on herself, stating: 'But worse to trust to my own mind / And find the same corruption there' (lines 23 to 24). Brontë, it seems, is adept at creating pitifully vulnerable characters of her speakers, and we see this again in the voice of 'Long Neglect Has Worn Away'. In a striking metaphor, the frail and aging speaker confesses to her own physical decay: 'Time has turned the bloom to grey; / Mould and damp the face defile' (lines 3 to 4), and we witness the vulnerability further as the now-withered speaker is pining for the 'Fair' (line 9) hand of her lost love – the youthful hand that wrote her compliments and 'Swiftly flew' (line 11) in the act. The irony of these images of youth further enforces the impact of time and the speaker's inability to return to younger, better days.

From here, we turn to the third key theme in our essay plan: 'settings'. We must read each poem again, however, and make notes accordingly. Here are some possible observations:

The setting in 'Spellbound' is a night scene in the harsh windy winter. The speaker is enthralled by the landscape it seems and enveloped by it. The natural world becomes intimidating and awe-inspiring too. The speaker is small in comparison, lost, yet subsumed by it. Next, the setting in 'The Visionary' is the silent house at night. All are asleep save the speaker of the poem, who waits for the mysterious figure to come to her. The wind is an important element here as are the snow and clouds and trees – images we have seen in 'Spellbound'. The nervous speaker is sensitive to the wind and the stirring air in the closing phases of the poem. Moving on, 'I Am the Only Being Whose Doom' does not give any explicit sense of the setting or landscape. This dramatic monologue gives a sense of a lone figure, perhaps in a quiet, private room – but it seems in all probability as if this is not enough for commentary in this section of the essay – therefore the poem will not feature in the commentary that follows. Finally, 'Long Neglect Has Worn Away' has a dramatic setting – it is a scene in which the speaker observes a portrait of a lost love. We have a vivid sense of the melancholic speaker, time-wearied, looking at these painful objects: the picture, the lock of hair, and the inscription or ('motto') which her lover once wrote for her.

With these notes on each poem in mind, here is an attempt at a more formal write-up. Note that we start with the poem 'Long Neglect Has Worn Away' because it feeds on smoothly from our last formal comments in the section on vulnerability:

> As we can see in Brontë's poems, the setting plays an important role and often has a direct relationship to the speaker, impacting on the mood and tone accordingly. For example, with 'Long Neglect Has Worn Away', we are left to imagine a quiet scene, in a private place where the reflective speaker intimately surveys the personal objects, the portrait and the hair, which remind her of her loss and of her dismal present state. The direct speech for the epigraph on line 10: '"Dearest, ever deem me true"' is an important moment of the poem, suggesting that the lone speaker dares to repeat these words, uttering them aloud in her privacy and solitude. This links to the dramatic setting which we see in 'The Visionary'. Once more we sense that the speaker is affected by both the privacy and solitude that she finds in the house while waiting for the mysterious figure to come to her. The hushed tones and the excitement of the speaker are contrasted to unsettling effect with the personified landscape. The speaker admits that while she undertakes her quiet vigil, she is left 'dreading every breeze / That whirls the wildering drift, and bends the groaning trees' (lines 3 to 4). The weather is an antagonist, the snow and wind are elements Brontë uses to disturb the scene – the 'snow-wreaths' are 'deep' (line 2) and the girl watches 'every cloud' (line 3) looming over, as she waits at the window looking out for the figure. There is even some relief on the speaker's part that the threatening winds can find no way in to blow out the candle (the 'guiding-star' of line 8) which will direct him across the wild landscape safely to her: 'Not one shivering gust creeps through pane or door; / The little lamp burns straight' (lines 6 to 7). In comparison, in the poem 'Spellbound', Brontë further personifies

> the weather, notably the wind, the cloudy skyscape, and the snow, to show both the awe-inspiring and terrifying impact that the fierce, deathly landscape can have on a person. In this case the speaker shares a relationship with the wild elements, succumbing to their mercy. We find a completely trapped, enthralled figure subject to the 'giant trees' which are 'bending' (line 5) down imposingly, under the storm which is 'fast descending' (line 7). We see Brontë grouping these suffocating images together for desired effect here, leading into the smothering repetitions in the final stanza: 'Clouds beyond clouds above me, / Wastes beyond wastes below' (lines 9 to 10).

After all this, at last, we are in a position to summarise the findings of our study. Here is an opportunity to conclude and evaluate the writer's craft, Brontë's central ideas, and the patterns and techniques which find their way across the different poems. Here then is an attempt at a meaningful conclusion:

> In conclusion, when exploring the speakers in a collection of Brontë's poems, we start to find a number of patterns forming. For example, she typically employs first-person speakers, placing them in vulnerable positions or in extreme isolation, to bring about great dramatic intensity. We see how Brontë is able to capture moments in time in poems like 'Spellbound' and 'The Visionary' where the two speakers find themselves consumed by their present moment entirely. These speakers are conflicted too, both emboldened yet frightened by the predicaments that each are faced with in the action of the poems accordingly. However, we also see Brontë create more reflective speakers in her poetry, most notably in 'Long Neglect Has Worn Away' and 'I Am the Only Being Whose Doom', where bleak negativity and stark pessimism are the driving forces in the respective works. Common to all poems in this collection is Brontë's ability to match mood and atmosphere with the character of the speaker. Therefore, all manner of places, be they the confines of a quiet room or the free and wild landscape, impact upon the speaker in question, bringing about a range of romantic questioning and existentialist thought. By doing this, Brontë is able to explore ideas of love, loss, identity, and the relationships that an individual shares, not only with other human beings, but also with the natural world.

Now, at this stage, in order to get a clear sense of the full essay, I advise once more going back to read only the formal essay paragraphs without the accompanying notes. This is made easier by the essay itself being written in a bold font. Try to sense how the essay structure and line of argument work throughout, from the introduction through to the conclusion.

Practice

Now that we have seen how to manage a number of poems by a single poet, we are in a position to practise ourselves.

As you might have noted, a lot of preparation goes into an essay composition of this sort and in many ways it feels like a great juggling act. However, there is nothing more rewarding for a reader of poetry than the close study of a single writer's work. It brings us closer to the given poet but it also gives us a greater general understanding of the particular poet's craft, skill, style, themes and interests.

So, in this final practice, we have four sonnets by William Shakespeare (1564–1616), four poems by Emily Dickinson (1830–1886) and four poems by the modernist poet, William Carlos Williams (1883–1963) with accompanying questions.

Remember to read the poems carefully and try to identify patterns and links between them, before deciding on the key themes which will make your essay come together.

How does Shakespeare present ideas about mortality in the four sonnets?

Sonnet 1

by William Shakespeare

> From fairest creatures we desire increase,
> That thereby beauty's rose might never die,
> But as the riper should by time decease,
> His tender heir might bear his memory:
> 5   But thou contracted to thine own bright eyes,
> Feeds thy light's flame with self-substantial fuel,
> Making a famine where abundance lies,
> Thy self thy foe, to thy sweet self too cruel:
> Thou that art now the world's fresh ornament,
> 10   And only herald to the gaudy spring,
> Within thine own bud buried thy content,
> And, tender churl, makes waste in niggarding:
>   Pity the world, or else this glutton be,
>   To eat the world's due, by the grave and thee.

146   *Exploring a Group of Poems*

Sonnet 10

by William Shakespeare

    For shame deny that thou bear love to any,
    Who for thyself art so unprovident.
    Grant, if thou wilt, thou art beloved of many,
    But that thou none loves is most evident:
5   For thou art so possessed with murderous hate,
    That 'gainst thy self thou sticks not to conspire,
    Seeking that beauteous roof to ruinate
    Which to repair should be thy chief desire.
    O! change thy thought, that I may change my mind:
10 Shall hate be fairer lodged than gentle love?
    Be, as thy presence is, gracious and kind,
    Or to thyself at least kind-hearted prove:
      Make thee another self for love of me,
      That beauty still may live in thine or thee.

Sonnet 14

by William Shakespeare

    Not from the stars do I my judgement pluck;
    And yet methinks I have Astronomy,
    But not to tell of good or evil luck,
    Of plagues, of dearths, or seasons' quality;
5   Nor can I fortune to brief minutes tell,
    Pointing to each his thunder, rain and wind,
    Or say with princes if it shall go well
    By oft predict that I in heaven find:
    But from thine eyes my knowledge I derive,
10 And, constant stars, in them I read such art
    As truth and beauty shall together thrive,
    If from thyself, to store thou wouldst convert;
      Or else of thee this I prognosticate:
      Thy end is truth's and beauty's doom and date.

Sonnet 19

by William Shakespeare

    Devouring Time, blunt thou the lion's paws,
    And make the earth devour her own sweet brood;

Pluck the keen teeth from the fierce tiger's jaws,
And burn the long-lived Phoenix in her blood;
5 Make glad and sorry seasons as thou fleets,
And do whate'er thou wilt, swift-footed Time,
To the wide world and all her fading sweets;
But I forbid thee one more heinous crime:
O, carve not with the hours my love's fair brow,
10 Nor draw no lines there with thine antique pen!
Him in thy course untainted do allow
For beauty's pattern to succeeding men.
    Yet do thy worst, old Time! Despite thy wrong
    My love shall in my verse ever live young.

How does Emily Dickinson present <u>feelings of despair</u> in her poetry?

I Felt a Funeral, in my Brain

by Emily Dickinson

I felt a Funeral, in my Brain,
And Mourners to and fro
Kept treading – treading – till it seemed
That Sense was breaking through –

5 And when they all were seated,
A Service, like a Drum –
Kept beating – beating – till I thought
My mind was going numb –

And then I heard them lift a Box
10 And creak across my Soul
With those same Boots of Lead, again,
Then Space – began to toll,

As all the Heavens were a Bell,
And Being, but an Ear,
15 And I, and Silence, some strange Race,
Wrecked, solitary, here –

And then a Plank in Reason, broke,
And I dropped down, and down –
And hit a World, at every plunge,
20 And Finished knowing – then –

It was not Death, for I stood up

by Emily Dickinson

It was not Death, for I stood up,
And all the Dead, lie down—
It was not Night, for all the Bells
Put out their Tongues, for Noon.

5   It was not Frost, for on my Flesh
I felt Sirocos—crawl—
Nor Fire—for just my Marble feet
Could keep a Chancel, cool—

And yet, it tasted, like them all,
10 The Figures I have seen
Set orderly, for Burial,
Reminded me, of mine—

As if my life were shaven,
And fitted to a frame,
15 And could not breathe without a key,
And 'twas like Midnight, some—

When everything that ticked—has stopped—
And Space stares all around—
Or Grisly frosts—first Autumn morns,
20 Repeal the Beating Ground—

But, most, like Chaos—Stopless—cool—
Without a Chance, or Spar—
Or even a Report of Land—
To justify—Despair.

There's a certain Slant of light

by Emily Dickinson

There's a certain Slant of light,
Winter Afternoons –
That oppresses, like the Heft
Of Cathedral Tunes –

5   Heavenly Hurt, it gives us –
We can find no scar,

But internal difference –
Where the Meanings, are –

None may teach it – Any –
10   'Tis the seal Despair –
An imperial affliction
Sent us of the Air –

When it comes, the Landscape listens –
Shadows – hold their breath –
15   When it goes, 'tis like the Distance
On the look of Death –

After great pain, a formal feeling comes

by Emily Dickinson

After great pain, a formal feeling comes –
The Nerves sit ceremonious, like Tombs –
The stiff Heart questions "was it He, that bore,"
And "Yesterday, or Centuries before"?

5   The Feet, mechanical, go round –
A Wooden way
Of Ground, or Air, or Ought –
Regardless grown,
A Quartz contentment, like a stone –

10   This is the Hour of Lead –
Remembered, if outlived,
As Freezing persons, recollect the Snow –
First – Chill – then Stupor – then the letting go –

How does William Carlos Williams present <u>the speaker</u> in his poems?

The Desolate Field

by William Carlos Williams

Vast and gray, the sky
is a simulacrum
to all but him whose days
are vast and gray, and—
5   In the tall, dried grasses

150   *Exploring a Group of Poems*

> a goat stirs
> with nozzle searching the ground.
> —my head is in the air
> but who am I...?

January

by William Carlos Williams

> Again I reply to the triple winds
> running chromatic fifths of derision
> outside my window:
> > Play louder.
> 5   You will not succeed. I am
> bound more to my sentences
> the more you batter at me
> to follow you.
> > And the wind,
> 10 as before, fingers perfectly
> its derisive music.

Complaint

by William Carlos Williams

> They call me and I go.
> It is a frozen road
> past midnight, a dust
> of snow caught
> 5   in the rigid wheeltracks.
> The door opens.
> I smile, enter and
> shake off the cold.
> Here is a great woman
> 10 on her side in the bed.
> She is sick,
> perhaps vomiting,
> perhaps laboring
> to give birth to
> 15 a tenth child. Joy! Joy!
> Night is a room
> darkened for lovers,
> through the jalousies the sun
> has sent one golden needle!

20 I pick the hair from her eyes
    and watch her misery
    with compassion.

Thursday

by William Carlos Williams

    I have had my dream—like others—
    and it has come to nothing, so that
    I remain now carelessly
    with feet planted on the ground
5 and look up at the sky—
    feeling my clothes about me,
    the weight of my body in my shoes,
    the rim of my hat, air passing in and out
    at my nose-and decide to dream no more.

Afterword

I hope that reading this book has introduced you to some of the important concepts in poetry criticism and to some of the great poets in the literary canon.

I sincerely hope that one or two of these poets have intrigued you enough to want to read more poetry in general. I write this because, beyond the immediate, academic function of the book, the point of all this is, after all, to encourage you, quite simply, to read more poetry!

Reading poetry improves lives. Reading poetry enriches lives.

I think that it is important, therefore, to remind students and readers alike that there is a wealth of poetry readily available to us, both for reading pleasure and the opportunity to study.

Poetry anthologies are a fine place to start for the generally intrigued: collections like *The Rattle Bag* (Faber and Faber), *The Oxford Book of English Verse* (Oxford University Press) or *The Norton Anthology of Poetry* (W.W. Norton and Company) are all excellent resources.

Poetry websites also offer a vast array of reading material and rich literary experiences. Think about credible poetry sites and foundations first of all and explore the archives of websites like *The Poetry Foundation* (www.poetryfoundation.org) and *The Poetry Society* (www.poetrysociety.org.uk). These are two of the most important and authoritative poetry sites.

If you utilise resources such as these, you might find that you discover a new poem or a poet and are left wanting more.

Who knows?

You might unearth a poem online or in a book that simply compels you.

Who knows?

When this happens, you might even be inspired to *write about* it!

Biographies of the Featured Poets

Moniza Alvi (1954–)
Alvi was born in Lahore, Pakistan, and came to England when she was a few months old. She grew up in Hertfordshire and studied at the universities of York and London. Her volumes have been shortlisted several times for the T S Eliot Prize. Alvi now tutors for the Poetry School.

Simon Armitage (1963–)
Armitage was born in 1963 in Yorkshire. In 1999 Armitage was named the Millennium Poet. In 2004 he was elected a Fellow of the Royal Society of Literature. Armitage was awarded the CBE for services to poetry in 2010 and presented with the Hay Medal for Poetry at the 25th Hay Festival in 2012. Armitage is the current national Poet Laureate (2019–2029).

Elizabeth Barret Browning (1806–1861)
Browning, a Victorian poet, is perhaps best known for her 'Sonnets From the Portuguese' ('How Do I Love Thee?' is one of the most famous) and 'Aurora Leigh'. She is also famous for her marriage to fellow poet, Robert Browning.

William Blake (1757–1827)
Blake was an English poet, painter, and printmaker. Largely unrecognised during his lifetime, Blake is now considered a seminal figure in the history of the poetry and visual arts of the Romantic Age.

Anne Bradstreet (1612–1672)
Bradstreet was the most prominent of the early English poets of North America and first writer in England's North American colonies to be published. She is the first Puritan figure in American Literature and notable for her large body of poetry, as well as personal writings published after her death.

Emily Brontë (1818–1848)
Brontë was an English novelist and poet who is best known for her only novel, *Wuthering Heights*, now considered a classic of English literature. She also

published a book of poetry with her sisters Charlotte and Anne titled *Poems by Currer, Ellis and Acton Bell*, with her own poems finding wide regard and acclaim with modern readers.

Robert Browning (1812–1889)
Browning was an English poet and playwright whose dramatic monologues put him among the foremost Victorian poets. Famous monologues of his are 'My Last Duchess' and 'Porphyria's Lover'. His poems are noted particularly for their strong characterisation.

John Clare (1793–1864)
Clare was an English poet. The son of a farm labourer, he became known for his celebrations of the English countryside and sorrows at its disruption. His poetry underwent major re-evaluation in the late 20th century and he is now often seen as a major 19th-century poet.

Emily Dickinson (1830–1886)
Dickinson was an American poet. Little known during her life, she has since been regarded as one of the most important figures in American poetry.

Imtiaz Dharker (1954–)
Dharker was born in Pakistan and brought up in Scotland. She is a British poet, artist, and video filmmaker. She has won the Queen's Gold Medal for her English poetry and was appointed Chancellor of Newcastle University from January 2020.

Paul Laurence Dunbar (1872–1906)
Dunbar was born on June 27, 1872, to freed slaves from Kentucky. He became one of the first influential Black poets in American literature, and was internationally acclaimed for his dialectic verse in collections such as *Majors and Minors* (1895) and *Lyrics of Lowly Life* (1896). 'Little Brown Baby' is one example of his dialect verse.

Thomas Hardy (1840–1928)
Hardy was an English novelist and poet. A Victorian writer, he was influenced both in his novels and in his poetry by Romanticism, including the poetry of William Wordsworth. He was highly critical of much in Victorian society, especially of the declining status of rural people in Britain.

Frances Ellen Watkins Harper (1825–1911)
Harper was an American poet, novelist, and journalist. She was also a prominent abolitionist and women's suffrage activist. She authored numerous books, including the poetry collections *Forest Leaves* (1845), *Poems on Miscellaneous Subjects* (1854), and several short stories.

Ted Hughes (1930–1998)
Hughes was an English poet, translator, and children's writer. Critics frequently rank him as one of the best poets of his generation, and one of the 20th century's greatest writers. He is particularly acclaimed for his nature poetry. He was appointed Poet Laureate in 1984 and held the office until his death.

Violet Jacob (1863–1946)
Jacob was a Scottish writer known for her vernacular poetry, which is written mainly in Scots dialect. She was described by a fellow Scottish poet Hugh MacDiarmid as 'the most considerable of contemporary vernacular poets'.

Elizabeth Jennings (1926–2001)
Jennings was an English poet whose works relate intensely personal matters in a plainspoken, traditional, and objective style and whose verse frequently reflects her devout Roman Catholicism and her love of Italy.

Ben Jonson (1572–1637)
Jonson was a Renaissance writer, playwright, and poet. A contemporary of Shakespeare, Jonson's craft exerted a lasting influence upon English poetry and stage comedy.

John Keats (1795–1821)
Keats was an English Romantic poet. He was one of the main figures of the second generation of Romantic poets, along with Lord Byron and Percy Bysshe Shelley. Some of his most acclaimed works are 'Ode to a Nightingale', 'To Autumn', and the famous sonnet 'On First Looking into Chapman's Homer'.

David Herbert Lawrence (1885–1930)
Lawrence was an English writer and poet. Predominantly a famous novelist, his collected works represent, among other things, an extended reflection upon the dehumanising effects of modernity and industrialisation. Lawrence's writing explores issues such as sexuality, emotional health, vitality, spontaneity, and instinct.

Charlotte Mew (1869–1928)
Mew was an English poet whose work spans the eras of Victorian poetry and Modernism. Notable poems are 'The Cenotaph' 'From a Window' and 'A quoi bon dire'.

Edna St Vincent Millay (1892–1950)
Millay was an American lyrical poet and playwright. Encouraged to read the classics at home, she was too rebellious to make a success of formal education, but she won poetry prizes from an early age, including the Pulitzer Prize in 1923, and went on to use verse as a medium for her feminist activism.

Sarojini Naidu (1879–1949)
Naidu was an Indian political activist and poet. She is known as an important campaigner in India's fight for independence, and a driving figure for civil rights, women's emancipation, and anti-imperialistic ideas. Her poetry is praised for its colour, imagery, and lyrical quality.

Wilfred Owen (1893–1918)
Owen was an English poet and soldier. He was one of the leading poets of the First World War. His war poetry on the horrors of trenches and gas warfare was much influenced by his mentor Siegfried Sassoon and stood in contrast to the public perception of war at the time and to the confidently patriotic verse written by earlier war poets such as Rupert Brooke.

Alice Oswald (1966–)
Oswald was trained as a classicist at New College, University of Oxford. Her first collection of poetry, *The Thing in the Gap Stone Stile* (1996), received a Forward Poetry Prize for Best First Collection. The poem 'Wedding' comes from this collection.

Katherine Philips (1632–1664)
Philips, also known as 'The Matchless Orinda', was an Anglo-Welsh royalist poet, translator, and woman of letters. She achieved renown as a translator of Pierre Corneille's *Pompée* and *Horace*, and for her editions of poetry after her death. She was highly regarded by many writers of 17th-century literature, including John Dryden and John Keats, as being influential.

Christina Rossetti (1830–1894)
Rossetti was an English poet who wrote various romantic, devotional, and children's poems. 'Goblin Market' and 'Remember' remain famous. She wrote the words of two Christmas carols well known in the UK: 'In the Bleak Midwinter' and 'Love Came Down at Christmas'. She was a sister of the artist and poet Dante Gabriel Rossetti, featuring in several of his paintings.

William Shakespeare (1564–1616)
Shakespeare was an English playwright, poet, and actor, widely regarded as the greatest writer in the English language and the world's greatest dramatist. He is often called England's national poet and the 'Bard of Avon'.

Edmund Spenser (1553–1599)
Spenser was an English poet best known for 'The Faerie Queene', an epic poem and fantastical allegory celebrating the Tudor dynasty and Elizabeth I. He is recognised as one of the premier craftsmen of Early Modern English verse, and is often considered one of the greatest poets in the English language.

Edward Thomas (1878–1917)
Thomas was a British poet, essayist, and novelist. He is considered a war poet, although few of his poems deal directly with his war experiences, and his career in poetry only came after he had already been a successful writer and literary critic. In 1915, he enlisted in the British Army to fight in the First World War and was killed in action during the Battle of Arras in 1917, soon after he arrived in France.

Jean Toomer (1894–1967)
Toomer was an American poet and novelist commonly associated with the Harlem Renaissance and modernism. An important figure in African-American literature, Toomer was the grandson of the first governor of African-American descent in the United States. Toomer's most famous work, *Cane*, was published in 1923 and was hailed by critics for its literary experimentation and portrayal of African-American characters and culture.

Anna Wickham (1883–1947)
Wickham was an English-Australian poet who was a pioneer of modernist poetry. She was friend to other important writers of the time, such as D. H. Lawrence Wickham lived a transnational, unconventional life, moving between Australia, England, and France. Her literary reputation has improved since her death and she is now regarded as an important early 20th-century woman writer.

William Carlos Williams (1883–1963)
Williams was a medical doctor, poet, novelist, essayist, and playwright. He was a leading poet of the Imagist movement and often wrote of American subjects and themes. He was known as an experimenter, an innovator, and a revolutionary figure in American poetry.

William Wordsworth (1770–1850)
Wordsworth was an English Romantic poet who, with Samuel Taylor Coleridge, helped to launch the Romantic Age in English literature with their joint publication *Lyrical Ballads* (1798). Wordsworth's magnum opus is generally considered to be 'The Prelude', a semi-autobiographical poem of his early years that he revised and expanded a number of times.

William Butler Yeats (1865–1939)
Yeats was an Irish poet and one of the foremost figures of 20th-century literature. A pillar of the Irish literary establishment, he helped to found the Abbey Theatre, and in his later years served two terms as a Senator of the Irish Free State. He was a driving force behind the Irish Literary Revival.

Glossary of Key Terms

addressee the figure addressed in the poem by the speaker.
adverb a word which describes a verb. These words often end in '_ly'.
alliteration repetition of the same consonant sound, especially at the beginning of words. For example, 'faltering forward'.
allusion a reference to a person, place, or incident outside the world of the text, or to another literary text.
anadiplosis a form of repetition in which the last word of one clause or sentence is repeated as the first word of the following clause or sentence.
anthropomorphism the attribution of human characteristics or behaviour to a god, animal, or object.
assonance echoed vowel sounds. For example, 'drip of it' is assonance on the short 'i' sound heard in the words 'drip' and 'it'. To identify assonance we must pay attention to short and long vowel sounds and the shape the mouth makes when uttering certain vowels.
ballad a form of verse, often narrative, often rhyming and set to music.
blank verse poetry written in unrhymed pentameter (or ten-syllable lines with five strong stresses).
caesura a pause in a line of poetry often made by some form of punctuation.
comparative adjective an adjective which shows a comparison. For example, words like 'bigger', 'stronger', 'better'.
conceit, or extended metaphor a series of linked images around a single idea that work on both the literal and metaphorical level.
conditional tense sometimes known as the hypothetical future tense. It is made by using the word 'If…' to speculate on or imagine future events.
continuous verbs verbs that end in '_ing'. These words, when accompanied by present tense auxiliary verbs create a sense of live, ongoing action in the 'moment' of the poem. For example 'Bees passing' and 'Bees returning'.
couplet a pair of verse lines. A 'rhyming couplet' is a pair of verse lines with rhyming end words. For example, 'For whose sake henceforth all his vows be such / As what he loves may never like too much'.
definite and indefinite articles the definite article is the word 'the', as in 'the chair' and indefinite articles are the words 'a' or 'an', as in 'a chair'.

Definite articles refer to specific nouns, while indefinite articles refer to general or non-specific nouns.

dialect   a particular form of a language which is peculiar to a specific region or social group.

dialogue   speech which is shared between two voices.

direct address   often identified by use of the 'you' pronoun, when the writer or the speaker addresses the reader or the addressee directly. For example, "You all have lied…."

direct speech   actual words that are spoken, identified by speech marks.

discourse markers   important words or phrases in the essay which create a line of argument.

dramatic monologue   a long speech by a sole voice.

end-stopped line   a line in poetry which is a complete sentence in itself, marked with a full stop at the end.

enjambment   a run-on line which continues into the next line.

elegy   a poem written to mourn the dead.

ellipsis   a punctuation mark, which suggests something is unfinished or left out, typically identifiable as three dots. For example, 'it blows like millions…'.

euphemistic language, or euphemism   language which is guarded or evasive, typically when dealing with sensitive, controversial, or taboo subjects.

feminine ending   a line of poetry which ends on a weakly-stressed syllable. Typically these are words ending in '_y', '_ly' or '_ing'.

first-person narrative perspective   where the speaker of the poem is identified by the 'I' pronoun.

free verse   a verse form which does not adhere to regular stanzaic or metrical patterns. In free-verse poetry we often find that stanzas are irregularly divided and that there is an interplay between long and short lines, and key moments of caesura and enjambment.

fricatives   a soft consonant sound. Words which start with 'f' or 'th', for example.

future tense   a verb tense which addresses the future by using auxiliary verbs like 'will' and 'shall'. For example, 'I will in her beauty rest'.

imperative   the mood or tone of a sentence which is directed by some form of demand, order, or instruction. For example, 'Remember me'.

lyric poem   a formal type of poetry which expresses personal emotions or feelings, typically spoken in the first person.

metaphor   a comparison of two elements by suggesting that one is like the other.

modal verb   an auxiliary verb that expresses necessity or possibility. Words like must, shall, will, should, would, can, could, may, might.

monologue   a speech spoken by a single voice.

monosyllabic lines   a line or phrase made up of words which each contain one syllable. These lines or phrases often slow down the speed of the poem. For example, 'There is no time to ask – he knows not what'.

octave a verse of eight lines. Traditional sonnets are often divided into an octave (eight lines) and a sestet (six lines).
onomatopoeia a sound-effect word which sounds like what it means. For example, 'drip' or 'splash'.
oxymoron the combination of two apparently opposite or contradictory terms. For example, 'lonely fair'.
pastoral a class of Romantic literature, where the scenic descriptions of nature are idyllic and far remote from the realities of any life, rustic or urban.
parentheses use of brackets around a word or phrase. Parentheses are used to show an afterthought, an aside or an interjection by the speaker, or perhaps to highlight an irony.
persona an imagined character as speaker of the poem. An example of this is the hawk in Ted Hughes's 'Hawk Roosting'.
personification the act of giving human qualities to inanimate objects or ideas.
plosives a particularly hard consonant sound on letters like t, k, and p.
pronoun a word that refers to participants in the discourse of a text. For example, I, you, he, she, it, we, they. Pronouns can be singular or plural.
prose written or spoken language in its ordinary form, without metrical structure.
quatrain a four-line stanza.
refrain repetition of a phrase, line, or series of lines throughout a poem.
rhetorical question a persuasive question which does not require answering because the answer is obvious or universally accepted.
rhyme the unity of sounds between words or their endings.
rhyme scheme the pattern of the rhyme throughout a poem. Often marked with capital letters as in the following examples: ABAB or ABCB, for example, where A denotes the first end-word, B denotes the next new rhyme, and C the next, etc.
sentence sense, or verse paragraphs the syntax of full sentences in the poem regardless of the lineation. Also called 'verse paragraphs'.
sestet six-verse lines. Traditional sonnets are often divided into octaves (the first eight lines) and sestets (the final six lines).
sibilance repeated 's' sounds throughout a line. Can be hard or soft.
stanza a group of lines separated from the rest. Stanza is the correct term for 'verse' in poetry.
simile a comparison between two elements using 'like' or 'as' (for example, 'She bid me take love easy / As the leaves grow on the trees').
sonnet a traditional love poem of fourteen lines.
speaker the voice of the poem.
stress the interplay between accented and unaccented syllables, or hard and soft syllables in a line.
superlative a word which denotes the best or worst of a kind. For example: best, worst, greatest, prettiest, ugliest, etc.

temporal adverbs adverbs which suggest some aspect of time. For example, now, then, after, etc.

third-person narrative perspective a poem which tells the story of someone else. The narrator is not usually involved directly. This perspective often relies on third person pronouns: 'he', 'she', 'it'.

time sense the verb usage in a poem. We identify past, present, or future tenses in this instance.

tone the type of voice the speaker uses and the attitude associated with the voice.

verse paragraphs the syntax of full sentences in the poem regardless of the lineation. Typically verse paragraphs are found in long blank verse poems.

volta the formal turning point in a sonnet. Usually this is found at the start of line 9 in traditional sonnets.

Index

alliteration 84, 92, 96, 109, 159
Alvi, Moniza 60–63, 154; 'An Unknown Girl' 60–63
anadiplosis 83, 159
anthropomorphism 28, 159
Armitage, Simon 56–60, 154; 'Zoom!' 56–60
assonance 95, 96, 159

Barret Browning, Elizabeth 98, 154; 'Sonnets from the Portuguese 43: How do I love thee? Let me count the ways' 98–99, 154
Blake, William 33–36, 40–42, 154; 'London' 33–36; 'Nurse's Song' 41–42
Bradstreet, Anne 124; 'To My Dear and Loving Husband' 124, 154
Bronte, Emily 135–145; 'I Am the Only Being Whose Doom' 136–145; 'Long Neglect has Worn Away' 137–145; 'Spellbound' 135, 137–145; 'The Visionary' 135–145
Browning, Robert 52–56, 154, 155; 'Home Thoughts from Abroad' 52–56

caesura 70, 73, 76, 78, 96, 107, 131, 159, 160
Clare, John 126–134, 155; 'Birds at Evening' 127–134; 'Open Winter' 126–134; 'Summer' 128–134; 'To the Fox Fern' 127–134
comparative adjective 56, 77, 159
conceit, or extended metaphor 36, 38, 39, 159
conditional tense 46, 83, 106, 159
continuous verbs 32, 38, 159
couplet 39, 47, 71, 73, 82, 84, 95, 159

Dharker, Imtiaz 93–98, 155; 'Blessing' 93–98
Dickinson, Emily 145, 147–149, 155; 'After great pain, a formal feeling comes' 149; 'I Felt a Funeral, in my Brain' 147; 'It was not for Death, for I stood up' 148; 'There's a certain Slant of Light' 148–149
direct address 5, 18, 92, 106, 109, 160
direct speech 9, 18, 20, 42, 46, 143, 160
discourse markers 106, 121, 160
dramatic monologue 29, 30, 137, 155, 160
Dunbar, Paul Laurence 112–121; 'Little Brown Baby' 113–121

elegy 102, 104, 107–109, 115, 116, 160
ellipsis 83, 160
end-stopped line 28, 95, 109, 160
enjambment 58, 76–78, 82–84, 96, 97, 160
euphemistic language, or euphemism 108, 160

feminine ending 82, 160
free verse 36, 37, 42, 56, 58, 60, 63, 93, 94, 97, 160
fricatives 96, 160
future tense 47, 55, 159, 162

Hardy, Thomas 4–8, 11–17, 22–23, 155; 'The Darkling Thrush' 11–17; 'The Ruined Maid' 23, 25; 'The Voice' 4–8
Harper, Frances Ellen Watkins 99–100, 155; 'Learning to Read' 99–100
Hughes, Ted 26–30, 39, 156, 161; 'Hawk Roosting' 26–30, 39

imperative 95, 116, 160
indefinite article 80, 159, 160

Index

Jacob, Violet 124–125, 156; 'Craigo Woods' 124–125
Jennings, Elizabeth 101–112, 156; 'For a Child Born Dead' 101–112
Jonson, Ben 112, 114–121, 156; 'On My First Son' 112–121

Keats, John 124–125, 156; 'To Ailsa Rock' 124–125

Lawrence, David Herbert 30–33, 40–42, 156, 158; 'Bat' 40–42; 'Piano' 30–33
lyric poem 49, 53, 56, 128, 160

metaphor 2, 15, 21, 34, 38–39, 52, 83, 95–98, 106, 107, 130, 131, 142, 160
Mew, Charlotte 124, 156; 'Rooms' 124
modal verb 47, 160
monosyllabic lines 37, 95, 160

Naidu, Sarojini 122–123, 157; 'Cradle Song' 122–123

onomatopoeia 58, 95, 161
Oswald, Alice 75, 81–85, 157; 'Wedding' 81–85
Owen, Wilfred 8–11, 17–25, 157; 'Conscious' 8–11; 'Disabled' 22–25; 'Inspection' 17–22
oxymoron 77, 78, 161

pastoral 128, 161
persona 28, 39, 161
personification 15, 21, 50, 91, 131, 134, 143, 161
Philips, Katherine 101–112, 157; 'On the Death of my First and Dearest Child' 101–112
plosives 109, 161

quatrain 82, 116, 161

refrain 68, 72, 80, 137, 140, 161
rhetorical question 106, 108, 109, 115, 119, 161
rhyme 1, 2, 74, 79–82, 85, 92, 109, 133, 161

rhyme scheme 2, 82, 161
Rossetti, Christina 65–74, 85–86, 157; 'No, Thank You, John' 85–86; 'Remember' 65–74

Shakespeare, William 15, 44–48, 53, 60, 61, 63, 82, 84, 123, 145–147, 156, 157; 'Sonnet 1' 145; 'Sonnet 2' 44–48; 'Sonnet 10' 146; 'Sonnet 14' 146; 'Sonnet 18' 123; 'Sonnet 19' 146–147; 'Sonnet 116' 61, 63
sibilance 79, 81, 96, 161
simile 79–84, 134, 161
sonnet 15, 44–46, 48, 49, 52, 53, 60, 61, 63, 65–68, 70–72, 74, 82, 84, 89, 90, 123, 128, 132, 145, 146, 156, 161, 162
Spenser, Edmund 123, 157; 'One day I wrote her name upon the sand' 123
stress 37, 91, 120, 159, 160, 161
St Vincent Millay, Edna 88–93, 156; 'Time does not bring relief' 88–93
superlative 120, 161

temporal adverbs 52, 54–56, 162
third-person narrative perspective 10, 11, 94, 98, 162
Thomas, Edward 75–78, 85, 86, 158; 'Adlestrop' 75–78, 85; 'Tears' 85, 86
Toomer, Jean 36–39; 'Beehive' 37–39

verse paragraphs 12, 44, 49, 58, 161, 162
volta 69, 83, 162

Wickham, Anna 122, 158; 'After Annunciation' 122
Williams, William Carlos 145, 149–151, 158; 'Complaint' 150–151; 'The Desolate Field' 149–150; 'January' 150; 'Thursday' 151
Wordsworth, William 48–53, 155, 158; 'Upon Westminster Bridge, September 3, 1802' 48–52

Yeats, William Butler 75, 78–81, 85–87, 158; 'Down by the Salley Gardens' 75, 78–81; 'The Lake Isle of Innisfree' 85–87

Printed in the United States
by Baker & Taylor Publisher Services